LIGHT THE COUNTRY FIRE

LIGHT

THE

COUNTRY FIRE

Karen Bokram and Sarah Young

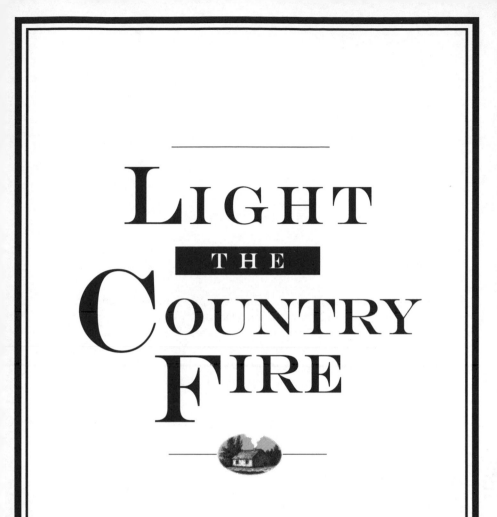

THE LYONS PRESS
Guilford, Connecticut
An imprint of The Globe Pequot Press

The Lyons Press is an imprint of The Globe Pequot Press.

Illustrations by Manuel F. Cheo
Design by Marcy Kass

10 9 8 7 6 5 4 3 2 1

Printed in the United States of America

ISBN 1-59228-112-5

Library of Congress Cataloging-in-Publication Data is available on file.

FOR OUR MOTHERS, JOAN AND CLAUDETTE,

WHO LIT THE FIRE SO LONG AGO

❧

FOR ALEXANDRA AND DANIEL

CONTENTS

ACKNOWLEDGMENTS

Sarah and I had a lot of help in writing this book and wish to thank all of the manufacturers, engineers, technicians, librarians, dealers, and most of all, all the woodstove and fireplace owners who shared their knowledge and experience with us.

In addition to them, we wish to thank some individuals and organizations who always were so helpful: Bob Armstrong of the Hearth Products Association, who arranged for me to attend the Hearth and Home Expo '93 and packed more information into two days than I ever thought possible (and thanks to all those who took time out to talk to a media person without leaving me mid-sentence for a customer); John Bittner of the National Chimney Sweep Guild; the Chimney Safety Institute of America; and Dave Johnston of Alternative Energy Retailer, who kept me so well informed. Thank you all.

This book would also not have been possible without a few other people—so in case we never get the chance again, thanks to Dr. Ulle Lewes, J.B.L., M.H., S.B., W.B., T.W., and all of our family and friends for their love and encouragement along the way.

—*Karen Bokram*

INTRODUCTION

Ever since the dawn of time, men have gathered around the fire for warmth and comfort. Even when castles and cottages replaced the cave, the fireplace served as a focal point for the home: Meals were prepared over the kitchen fire, families gathered around fireplaces in the public rooms to talk and tell stories of adventure, and fireplaces in the bedrooms provided heat as well as a warm glow to fall asleep by.

With the advent of cookers and central heating, houses no longer required a fireplace in every room—or a fire master to keep the home fires burning. As a result, many people don't know the art of making a fire or creating a wonderful fireplace for their home. And more importantly, many families haven't experienced the joy of gathering around a crackling fire to enjoy guests or each other.

Fires mesmerize us, relax us, warm us, soothe us, give us a sense of wonder. Fires are romantic, comforting, mysterious, and primal. They can be as beautiful as they are savage.

We hope to bring the joy of fires back to your home and family and allow you to rediscover a pleasure of the past.

—*Sarah Young and Karen Bokram*

1

SEEING THE FOREST
FOR THE TREES:
All about wood

Wood is a vital part of our lives. Perhaps you haven't thought about it in a while but take a second to remember all the great things that wood makes possible: We build our homes with it, print our newspapers on it, read our faxes off it, commute to work over wooden railroad ties, and sit at desks and chairs carved of the stuff. And that's not even counting all the chemicals and by-products wood provides us with. There is not a single day when wood doesn't play an important part in our lives.

Wood, obviously, can also be used to heat our homes or can simply be burned for our enjoyment. For some reason or another, burning wood has gotten a bum rap. Despite the trend back to heating with wood (thanks to the oil crisis some years back and an increasing desire for self-sufficiency), there are those well-meaning, "environmentally conscious" city dwellers that show up at your house on weekends and start telling you how your woodstove or fireplace is destroying the forest and polluting the air. However, when considering woodburning, we aren't talking about lighting up with redwoods or evicting some owl out of its rightful home; we're talking about deriving energy from a renewable natural resource.

Let us say now that we love the forest and all the furry things that live there. We love trees from roots to leaf tips, chlorophyll to critters. We do not advocate clear-cutting of forests in any country (and rest assured that clear-cutting is not done for the purpose of harvesting wood) and do not advocate irresponsible land management. We encourage all woodburners to comply with EPA standards and obey local burn laws and make sure their equipment (be it woodstove or fireplace or any other burning appliance) is being operated in a responsible manner.

For those people who think that woodburners are depleting our forests, here are a few facts.

In order for woodburning to have a serious impact on our forests, Americans would have to choose wood as opposed to all our other natural energy sources (oil, coal, electricity). Despite rising bills, this isn't likely to happen. (What could happen is that one day we run out of these non-renewable resources, but even then other alternatives like solar energy would be far more useful on a mass scale.)

Second, we have become much more conscious about how our homes use energy. Certainly concern is not totally misplaced. Five hundred years ago, much of western Europe was dense forest. But as the population grew, the woods were slowly depleted as wood was required to warm the castle halls. Well, here in America in the 1990s, drafty bell towers have been replaced by attics with 3′-thick fiberglass. We've insulated our homes and become energy conscious to the point that it now takes just a fraction of the energy it took to heat our homes fifty years ago.

Third, our woods are constantly being reforested. While we certainly must be diligent to this end, we lose much more valuable natural land to highways and cities and real estate development than we ever do to woodburning. (If you really want to get mad, consider the developer who thinks Walden Woods is a fabulous place for condos.)

Wood, with proper respect, is most likely an infinite fuel. With proper care of our existing tree supply, reforestation, a cessation of wasteful lumbering and the continuation of recycling, there remains no reason not to burn in a responsible manner.

As far as pollution is concerned, laws set out by the Environmental Protection Agency (EPA) have regulated woodstoves for some time now and the 1990s have represented an era in which air pollution from woodstove-burning has diminished greatly. Each year brings a new crop of stoves that spew a minimum of by-products into the air (we're talking clean in the 80–90% range). Local areas vulnerable to pollution have also imposed burning regulations that have limited the amount of pollutants in the air and improved its quality dramatically. Quite simply, woodburning—when done properly—does not expel a significant amount of pollution into the atmosphere.

KINDS OF WOODS AND GETTING THEM

There are a lot of different types of trees out there, but when you talk about trees for woodburning, you divide them into two basic types—hardwoods and softwoods. Hardwoods are found predominantly in the northern and midwestern parts of the United States and softwoods basically in the South.

For longer burning with more heat output, hardwoods are where it's at. Softwoods, with the exception of tamarack, are best used only for kindling (see chart).

Now once you know what kind of wood you're after (mostly hard with a little softwood for kindling), you have only two choices as to how you get it. You can (a) be conventional and have it delivered or (b) re-create all your Abe Lincoln Fantasies and select, saw, haul, and split it all yourself.

We've done both. Allow us to say that if you've got a nice, sunny 50° spring afternoon, a pack of strong, outdoorsy friends, and a supply of shiny chainsaws and axes, you might have enough wood by the end of the day to last you, if you're lucky, a few winter weekends. For a moment, let's assume that it's fall, you've heard that a noreaster is expected, and the woodpile consists of about twenty soggy logs that your kid kicked over last week playing hide-and-seek. This is where a delivery of wood comes in very handy.

Believe it or not, most states require wood to be sold in measurement units. When talking to a wood dealer, he'll ask you how much you want. "A lot" is not considered to be a good answer here. He'll most likely be looking for you to be talking about cords. There is such a thing as a standard cord. This is a pile of wood stacked four feet high and eight feet wide with logs that are four feet long. What most people want is what's called a face cord or short cord. The pile is the same height (4') and same width (8') but the logs are only 1–2' long. There is also such a thing as a long cord (4' high, 8' wide, with logs that are longer than 4') and finally, a unit (a stack that measures 2' high, 2' wide, with logs that are 16" long—the bundle you pay $10 for in large cities in winter).

While the dimensions might vary a bit, a standard cord should come out to 128 cu. ft. of wood, and should weigh about 2 tons. (Just in case you had ideas about taking the Explorer to the wood lot and avoiding the delivery charge, think again.)

WOOD CHART

Here is a list of the general types of wood best suited to burning. All wood should be seasoned. (Wood is called "green" when it is first cut and "seasoned" after it has been left to dry until its moisture content is about 20%. This can take six months to a year.)

These are hardwoods. Some softwoods you can consider for kindling are pine, fir, and spruce. As we mentioned, tamarack also has value as a burning wood. Of course, the output of these woods depends on your woodburning appliance, how well the wood is seasoned, etc. but this should give you an idea of what you're dealing with. Be forewarned that elm and sycamore are a pain to split. Unless a professional splits them for you, it's best to pass them up. Unless, of course, your other alternative is freezing—then swing away.

WOOD	SPLITABILITY	SPARKS	SMOKE	NOTES
Apple	Difficult	Light	Light	Smells really good
Ash	Average	Moderate	Light	Can be used green
Beech	Can be difficult	Light	Light	Seasons best split
Birch	Average	Moderate	Light	Split immediately, will decay
Elm	Very difficult	Light	Moderate	
Hickory	Can be difficult	Light	Light	Very heavy wood
Ironwood (Hardhack)	Difficult	Light	Light	Must be split green
Maple	Average	Light	Light	
Maple sugar	Can be difficult	Moderate	Light	
Oak, red	Average	Light	Light	
Oak, white	Can be difficult	Light	Light	
Shagbark	Can be difficult	Light	Light	

LIGHT THE COUNTRY FIRE

Identifying different types of wood.

Softwoods	Hardwoods

pine

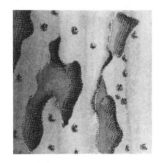

apple

fir (balsam)

maple

black spruce

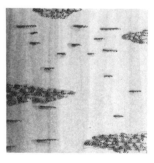

birch

Before you even pick up the phone to call the dealer, get a sense of what woods are local—these should be your best value. If you don't really know, just call up and say you want a full cord of seasoned firewood, that only oak and hickory are acceptable, though apple, maple, and elm are okay, too (this is what the in-the-know customers say), and that you want the wood delivered and neatly stacked.

Dealers have varying charges for delivered and stacked cords and all we can tell you is that we've found prices ranging from $80 to $200, depending on the type of wood, whether it's seasoned or unseasoned, cut into short logs, etc. The important thing is to be sure that you know what you are getting. Say that a standard or long cord is okay and you'll be sawing four-foot logs in the dead of winter. If the dealer offers to "deliver" the wood, you may come home to a two-ton pile of wood that's been dumped rather unceremoniously at the end of your driveway.

Some dealers also sell "mixed" cords. These cords can be either a variety of hardwoods or a combination of hard and soft woods. Be sure you know the contents and how the breakdown is done before you order. If you plan on starting a lot of fires (which is to say that you aren't going to be constantly feeding an existing fire and will have to start quite a few from scratch), you might want to have your woodpile be up to 20% soft wood. But again, be sure of what you're getting.

As with anything you buy, it pays to shop around. Call different dealers to see what kind of prices you can get. If you can plan far enough ahead, and can buy in the spring or summer, as opposed to late fall and winter, you'll have better-seasoned wood and a better price.

Once you've settled on the wood and the terms of delivery, try to arrange a time when you can be present for the delivery. One dealer showed up with a "truckload" of wood that he tried to sell at the cord price. He said it was "about" a cord. We demonstrated for him that a standard pickup can hold only about a third to half a full cord and then showed him the door.

Assuming that the load is honest, you next want to be sure the wood is stacked properly. Properly means that all the pieces of wood are stacked parallel to each other, except at each end, where they should be "pen stacked" (each end stacked in a square to hold the entire pile together). You also should give it a light kick. If the pile tumbles over, politely ask them to try again—tell them you prefer not to have the whole thing come down the first time you lift out a log.

You should also inspect a few pieces to make sure it is the wood you ordered (think back to learning tree identification in third grade, or if this doesn't work, refer to the chart on page 18) and that it is indeed seasoned. As we said before, you'll want to buy "seasoned" firewood (wood that has been cut and dried to 20% moisture) unless you have the time (about six-plus months) to season it yourself (and it should

Unseasoned wood   Seasoned wood

be cheaper if you buy the wood unseasoned). We'll explain shortly how to do so.

To check if wood has been seasoned, first check the heaviness. Wood that hasn't been seasoned is about 60% water and thus quite heavy. Wet logs also make a dull thud when struck together (as opposed to dry logs, which make a sound like a snap). But the easy way to know is by looking at the cut end of a piece. Seasoned wood should show radiating spokes that are similar to the spokes of a wheel. These cracks appear as the wood dries. Should the pieces be tightly packed, without cracks, the wood is still green and is not acceptable in this case. (If you are in the woods and have to cut whatever is available, green wood can quickly become acceptable: It will kick out close to the same heat but won't light as easily and will shoot a significant amount of creosote—those dangerous deposits of wood by-products—up your chimney.)

But say you want to forgo paying someone to drop the stuff neatly at your doorstep, all nicely stacked, trimmed, and dried. Times are tough and there is a lot of free heat just lying around for the asking. You just have to go get it.

The first place to check, of course, is your own property. We're not suggesting you take the saw to that great oak that has sat in the front yard for generations. Somewhere out back you probably have a wooded area chock full of trees that are dead or dying. Go after those first.

Should you not be fortunate enough to have some land, talk to a friend who has an acre or two—preferably talk to them after a good storm. Ask them if they have any fallen trees that might need to be removed. Tell them that you realize such wood impedes the growth of other trees and vegetation, and instead of their hiring someone to haul it away, you'll come get it for free, being the nice friend that you are. It may not be the best wood for burning, especially if it's at all rotten, but it's free and waiting for you. If you really win the tree lottery, however, you might find some trees that have been lying in wait and are already seasoned and only surface-wet.

We even know people who approach others in the community who aren't likely to forage for themselves, namely the elderly or weekenders who don't burn much. Offer your free cleanup services around, and who knows what you might find.

You can also find a real bonanza with the telephone and utility companies. How many times have you seen a crew trimming or cutting trees that interfere with service? This should be your cue to hop out of the car and offer to haul away this fallen wood; they'll be only too happy to hold the wood while you get your truck, and God knows they don't mind someone else doing their cleanup work for them. If you don't want to be so "catch-as-catch-can" about it, you might want to call and ask when they have scheduled the next tree-trimming operation in your neighborhood.

If you are really extra lucky, you might be fortunate enough to have some lines going up in your area. The power and phone companies cut a path several yards wide for new installations and will fell everything, no matter how nice the tree. With some muscle, you can haul away tons of free firewood. And, again, they are only too happy to let you do it.

Others who are all too happy to let you clean up are the town administrators. After storms, they often remove fallen trees and set them to the side. Yours for the taking.

It also pays to check the town dump after a bad storm. Many times homeowners, utility companies, and property managers bring fallen trees to the dump, and—here's the good part—they most likely have already chopped the trees into manageable pieces. Plus who knows what else you might find…

One of the best sources for free wood is the state or national park or forest near you. Like any place else, these reserves have trees that must be removed for safety reasons as well as for the health of the forest. Authorities permit people to come in and remove anything they like from certain specially marked areas, usually for free or for a nominal charge (we found some permits costing a whole $4). Be sure to call ahead to find out your park's policy and the best time to come.

Another potential gold mine is your local sawmill, furniture company, or lumberyard. As with any other business, these places have scrap left over and rejects that are unusable to them. Call up and offer to cart their extras away. If they've become aware of the hidden asset they may have previously been giving away, they may charge you a bit, but rest assured, it will be a lot less than what a dealer would charge. If you are charged, be sure that it's wood you can use (these industries utilize a good deal of softwood).

Another person who will have extra wood at a really low price is your local orchard owner. There are a lot of apple orchards near us and they call when they're pruning trees or replacing unproductive ones (we love the smell of applewood in the fire). While you may pay a small fee for the right to haul this wood away, fruitwoods burn well and smell wonderful. They're certainly worth a trip and a few dollars.

If you are a serious woodburner with any eye toward self-sufficiency and you own a bit of land, you may want to start your own woodlot. Tree farms are essentially just heavily wooded areas that are carefully managed. Maintaining a woodlot is not as hard as you might imagine, but you will want to enlist the help of your local forester and consult some of the books available on the subject (check your library).

HOW TO STORE YOUR WOOD

Congratulations! If you've gotten this far, you are now probably the proud owner of a big lump-o'-logs. So now what? Well, first you should figure out if you're going to have to cut any of these logs down to size. If you've gotten a face cord delivered, that answer would probably be a negative. If you bought a standard cord, a long cord, or secured the wood yourself, it's probably occurred to you by now that you're going to have to face some serious log-splitting.

Sawing and splitting logs is not especially difficult work. And as long as you know how to do it properly and safely, it isn't even especially dangerous work. In order to do it, you need to start out with the two basics—a chainsaw and an ax. You'll also need a maul (an ax/sledgehammer hybrid), a chopping block (a stump can sub for one of these), and a sawhorse if you want to be really proper about it (though two logs laid on the ground are known to work, too). An eight-pound sledgehammer and some eight-pound wedges should round out your wood-chopping ensemble.

Assuming you actually own these things, we will also assume you know what to do with them. We cannot stress enough the importance of knowing both how to use this equipment safely and how to outfit yourself properly (noise, flying wood, and a bad swing can all cause life-altering mishaps). If this is uncharted territory for you, we encourage you to seek out a master who can spend an afternoon showing you the ropes. He or she will teach you not only how to buck (the technical term for turning wood into firewood) properly, but also probably how to do so without taxing every single muscle in your body.

We know how to do this ourselves but we've elected not to give you a step-by-step here. Instead, we are so concerned about your safety that we feel you should be taught in person, by someone with many years of experience. Bucking is a time-honored art and, like any art, should be learned through apprenticeship.

Creating a woodpile is another time-honored art. A good woodpile can survive an earthquake, while an inferior one will tumble at the slightest provocation (like removing a log).

Start your woodpile by first seeing how dry the wood is. If it's wet, you'll want to leave room for air to circulate (plan on stacking in a crisscross pattern, making X's as you build). If it's dry, plan on building a tightly stacked pile with "pen stacked" ends as previously mentioned.

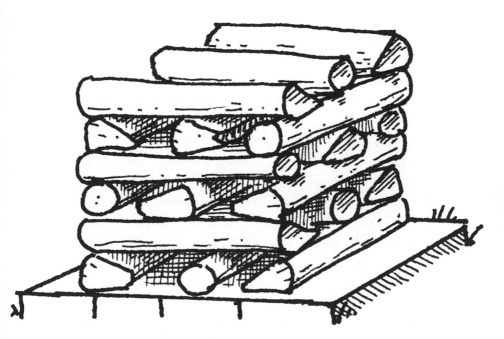

If your wood is wet, stack the logs in a criss-crossed fashion, leaving room for air to circulate. This speeds the drying process.

Next, determine whether you want to build your pile indoors or outdoors. The argument for storing wood indoors is that it not only makes those late-night woodbox refills easier to bear, but the wood fares much better where it's warm and dry. The argument against storing wood indoors is that it will rot quicker when kept at 60–90°. Rot begins at the bottom of a pile and continues up, so it's important to rotate the logs every once in a while and check often for signs. The best thing to do is build your pile on a foundation of bricks or boards, as opposed to right on the ground. Also be sure that whatever is serving as the base for this pile can take the weight (remember, two *tons*). Some good places to store wood are on a sun porch, in a cellar, in an unused sunroom, a free space in the garage, or the corner of a mud room.

Or you can put your woodpile outdoors, which is what most people end up doing. If you really luck out, the person who built your house might have also thought to put up a woodshed. A friend of ours has a woodshed that is one hundred years old and still as solid as the day it was put up. If you want to recreate a bit of Americana, it doesn't take more than some old boards to create a lean-to that will double for the same purpose.

If you don't have a woodshed, try to place the stack under your porch, overhang, or outside staircase, but do try to keep it at least six inches away from the house—critters and bugs tend to take residence in woodpiles and you don't want them to destroy the side of your house. If it's possible, place the pile near an operable window so you can just hand the logs in and avoid trekking back and forth (and think of all the energy you'll save by not having to leave the door open).

If you end up just building the pile out in the open, remember that you'll have to cover it. The popular thing around our town is to blanket woodpiles with blue plastic (and hospital corners), but let us assure you that's about the worst thing you can do. Blue plastic is truly ugly; and, more importantly, wrapping your woodpile like a Christmas present will choke off the air and sunlight it needs for proper aging and trap the moisture you're so desperately trying to get rid of. Take the top off and let the poor thing breathe a bit. Create a tent that protects the top and sides but allows several inches of breathing room.

Now that you've figured out the how and where, grab a few logs and start building. You're aiming for straightness and solidity, making sure the pile holds steady and doesn't lean. You can construct several small towers that lean on one another or go for the brass ring of woodpile-building, several crisscrossed stacks. (Be sure to separate the hardwoods and softwoods if you have a mixed pile; there's nothing worse than trying to chink out that single piece of pine.)

However you end up stacking, you have to have a brace at the ends. Sometimes this comes in the form of a wall or a side of the shed, but some people like to go fancy and buy one of those iron forms that allows you to make a tidy woodpile.

Once you've built your woodpile—and taken a few minutes to pat yourself on the back and soak all those muscles that are probably screaming at you by now—be sure to check its steadiness once in a while. Logs do shrink and shift as time goes on. As you take logs for the fire, be sure to work your way across the woodpile, not down. Not only will that keep your pile solid, but it will make sure the wood is uniformly dry, giving you a more consistent burn.

2

ALL ABOUT CHIMNEYS

HOW A CHIMNEY WORKS

Chimneys seem like such simple things. So simple that when our toddlers first started drawing, all the houses (which for them were a box with a triangle on top) had a sturdy-looking "chimney" at the side. It's only as home-owning adults that we learn appearances are deceiving.

Americans own roughly 40 million or so fireplaces, and they all operate on the same two principles—isolation and convection.

Isolation basically means that the fire you make in your fireplace won't choose to make an unescorted tour of the rest of your house. The combustion (or conversion of your solid materials, i.e., wood, to by-products like smoke and ash) is contained in your fireplace by the use of fireproof masonry.

The process of convection allows the smoke from the fire to wander up the chimney. It explains why fires, though toasty while you're seated close to them, really suck all the heated air out of the house. Convection works because of something called a flue. The flue is the inner part of the chimney through which the fireplace is vented (the

28

"chimney" is technically just the outer casing of the flue that you see sticking out of the roof.) The flue is also the part that you look up to see if the damper (a unit that serves as a little door or lid to control the draft in the flue passage) is open.

The flue creates a draft that, if everything is going well, causes the smoke to drift up the chimney. However, the air that creates the draft by going up the flue must be replaced by air in the room, which in turn must be replaced by air from outside. Unfortunately, fireplaces operate at about 10% or so efficiency, which means that 90% of the heat from the wood goes up the flue. The cold-air intake basically offsets the gain from woodburning.

The process we just described to you is what happens when chimneys are operating under perfect conditions. Loosely translated, that means nothing in the entire construction is in less-than-perfect condition, and the person who designed it took advantage of optimal draft conditions, and the person who constructed it made all the proper calculations and used the best materials. If this describes your fireplace, congratulations. But if you're like us, you've probably managed to purchase a home with more style and character than intelligence (we're tempted to start talking about the design of our kitchens here, but you get the idea), and you've found yourself with problems.

Like a fireplace that burps smoke in your face for no reason.

Or smoke that starts to seep out of places other than the top of your chimney.

Or you find yourself, despite our hints, unable to get a good blaze going (you never knew you could blame this on the chimney, did you?).

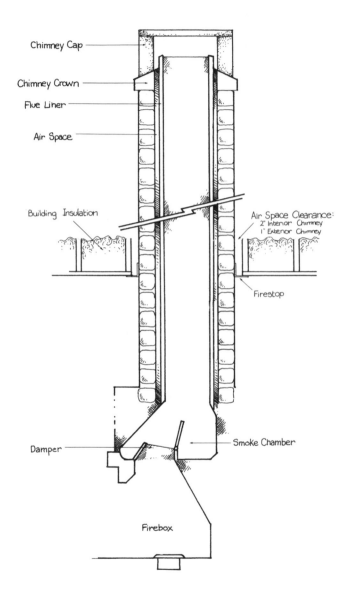

Parts of a chimney

FIREPLACE PROBLEMS AND CHIMNEY SOLUTIONS

Solutions to fireplace problems vary as widely as what causes them, so it's important to understand their nature and what to do about them. The trouble signs you're getting now should be heeded because they may be indicators that your chimney is at risk to catch fire—a problem that isn't as easily remedied as some described here.

INTERMITTENT PUFFING

At best, occasional smoking from your fireplace can be credited to a wind problem. This happens when high winds find their way down the flue and into the fire box, causing the smoke to reroute back into

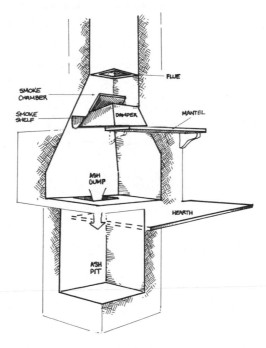

Parts of a fireplace

the room. This usually occurs in traditional masonry chimneys. If you live in a windy area, you might want to invest in a chimney cap. Not only do chimney caps minimize the draw of high winds, but they keep any woodland creatures from making a home atop yours (another cause of backsmoking).

If you live in a house roofed with flammable shingles, or in a heavily wooded area, the addition of a spark-guard is a must. Chimney caps with this feature keep sparks from escaping and landing on the roof or in the yard. Because wire mesh is a magnet for leaves and other debris, do a periodic visual check to be sure that yours is clear.

Also be aware that living under a canopy of conifers can cut the draft as well. Trim back any branches at least 15' from the chimney. Should any sparks fly, this trimming will not only decrease the chance of a forest fire among your firs, but it will increase the draft.

Air circulation can be a problem inside your house as well. Air leaks can cause changes in air pressure and draftiness, contributing to the smoke's being drawn back into the room. Particularly on windy days, heat escaping out loose-fitting doors and windows can suck air from the fireplace. Caulking and weatherstripping is a good idea in general and will eliminate the internal draft problem. It's also a good idea to close all the upstairs windows and doors to reduce the draw effect.

STEADY SMOKING

This is a slightly tougher problem. Your first task is to determine if your chimney is drawing at all. Light a piece of kindling and see whether there is any smoke going up the flue. If not, logic would tell us, something is blocking the flow of air. Grab a flashlight and take a look at the walls of the flue. Are they layered with a black fuzz or a slick thick enough to hamper air flow? (The layer should never be more than ¼″—if it is, don't attempt to light anything again until the chimney has been cleaned; you have a disaster waiting to happen.)

Also check to see that flue tiles have not fallen, thus causing a block. If any have fallen, a chimney fire has probably occurred without your knowing it. While free-burning chimney fires announce themselves with a vengeance, smaller, slow-burning chimney fires can pass unnoticed until you happen across the remains. Should you find any indicators of a chimney fire (more on that in a minute), don't use the fireplace again until you get it inspected and repair the flue.

Next, try to check for signs of furry residents lodging in the penthouse. Look around the firebox for any predictable signs, then shine your flashlight around the chimney for any signs of nesting materials. If you can manage to inspect the top of your chimney without risking life and limb, do so.

Assuming that the flue is clear, check the air pressure within the house. First, crack a window on the windward side of the house near the fireplace. This should provide the proper draft to put smoke up the chimney. Also be sure that no kitchen or bathroom exhaust fans are in operation and check that you remembered to shut down any attic fans for the season (you'd be amazed how many times this escapes notice).

If you have forced heat, check that vents and return-air registers aren't blocked. Air pressure can become imbalanced should the incoming air vents be blocked, thus forcing the return air—and fireplace smoke—to get drawn back toward the furnace. A badly designed forced-air system also can be the culprit if too much return air is routed through oversized return-air registers. In either case, the fireplace will smoke constantly when you're pumping hot air into the house. You may need to call someone in to resize the return-air ducts.

If you still can't locate the source of the trouble, things might be more complicated than your merely having to rearrange some air—but try these final checks.

Leaky trap door Some fireplaces come equipped with something called an ash trap, an opening in the bottom of the fireplace that allows the ashes to fall into a container in the basement. This trap door is supposed to be airtight, but if it isn't, an updraft can be sending the smoke back in the room.

Other fireplaces in the house Houses that have more than one fireplace are a joy unless you have a draft that is sucking smoke from one fireplace to the other. This results in something called the "stack effect." If upper-story fireplaces aren't being used, it's best to seal them off so you don't smoke out the one downstairs that is in use. If you do use your upstairs fireplace—what better than to enjoy a roaring blaze on a rainy Sunday afternoon while you're tucked under the covers watching football or reading a mystery—fit it with glass doors.

If you need a quick solution to the stack effect, crack a downstairs window to shift the air around. To correct the problem permanently, you'll need to install air-intake pipes into the firebox (there are kits for doing this, while those of us less handy can get the work done by a chimney sweep).

Design problems If you have done all this and are still experiencing problems, you are probably the victim of bad design and have our sincerest sympathies as fellow survivors of inadequate planning on the part of builders.

First look at the height of your chimney. Aside from being an escape route for smoke, chimneys are designed to draw the draft up into the fireplace to keep the flames fanned. Adequate chimney height and proper clearance from other parts of the roof are crucial for producing a proper draft and for making sure that all of the sparks from the fire have a chance to be rendered harmless.

Most builders abide by the "3-2-10" rule to figure the proper height for a chimney. Translated to layman's terms that means the chimney must be at least three feet higher than the highest part of the roof opening through which the chimney passes and at least two feet higher than any part of the roof within ten feet of the chimney exit. If your chimney doesn't meet these requirements (we've found this happens a lot when a budget-minded former owner puts a new addition too close to the original structure), the draft will be inadequate. We'd love to tell you there's an easy solution for this, but except for moving and keeping this little tidbit to yourself until after you've closed, it's a grim situation. It's best to let the pros take over from here, so consult with your architect and builder.

The other potential design blunder lies with multiple exterior chimneys. Should the chimneys be located too close to one another, smoke can find its way from one chimney to another when only one chimney is in use (this usually happens when the flue of the inactive fireplace is left open.) If this happens a lot (wind shifts can occasionally help you cheat this), you may have to seal off the top of one of your flues.

Flue Linings Speaking of flues and things that can go wrong, linings rank right up there. Defined as "a clay, ceramic, or metal conduit installed inside of a chimney, intended to contain the combustion products, direct them to the outside atmosphere, and protect the chimney walls from heat and corrosion," a flue lining can be your best friend or worst nightmare, depending on how lucky you get.

Your luck may run out before you even get started. Though codes and building practices vary, installing a flue lining has been de rigueur since the early part of this century. Nonetheless, many people went ahead anyway and put up a system without one (an act deemed by the 1940s National Bureau of Standards—the government types paid to busy themselves with such matters—as something a "little less than criminal"). Which means you have to start from scratch.

But suppose for a moment that the house fairy has smiled on you and you do have some raw material to work with. How can you tell if your flue is okay? In a perfect situation, you have a chimney sweep come in and evaluate any chimney that is unfamiliar to you so that you can be sure it's safe; but should you find yourself house hunting or, even better, invited to stay the month at your brother's condo in Steamboat, it's essential to know the signs of a faulty flue. Why? Because a damaged flue probably means one thing—that a chimney fire occurred and no one has replaced the damaged parts. For someone buying a house, that adds thousands of dollars in repair costs to get the thing working.

First, check to see that the chimney does indeed have a flue. If it doesn't, the material you see on the outside of the chimney will be the same as that on the inside, usually brick. You might as well stop right here. If the chimney has no lining, it's unsafe, since unlined chimneys allow heat to move through their brick walls very quickly. In tests, unlined chimneys cause adjacent woodwork to catch fire after only three-and-a-half hours.

Hopefully you'll look up into the firebox and find a lining of some sort, probably clay tile. Being a ceramic product, clay won't crack from normal usage, but it will crack from thermal shock.

Thermal shock happens when there is a rapid rise in temperature, as when you have any kind of chimney fire. The extreme temperature from a chimney fire will heat the inside of the tile very rapidly and cause it to expand—so quickly, in fact, that the outside of the tile doesn't have time to catch up, and it will split and crack until the tile just blows apart.

Fortunately or unfortunately, the signs of thermal shock are pretty obvious and any of them should have you reconsidering the wisdom of the "fireplace bear-rug" scenario or of putting in any bid that doesn't have provisions for fireplace repair.

First, ashes from burned creosote are usually present after a chimney fire. The ashes will be different from what you are used to—steel-gray in color, they'll be lightweight and fragile and they'll look like tissue paper. They'll also have a distinctly peculiar odor that defies any description we can think of.

Second, you might notice really clean areas appearing at random in the flue. This means that certain parts have been hit with extremely high heat and there are possible air leaks into the chimney (and that pretty much means your chimney is rotting out from the acidic flue gases).

Third, metal components such as dampers, chimney caps, or metal smoke chambers may be warped and/or discolored. Antennas mounted near the chimney might also show signs of damage.

Finally, check to see that the header (the part between the top of the firebox and the mantel) and any other surrounding areas show no signs of smoke damage. Unless a complete repatch job was done to conceal a chimney fire, you'll be able to notice gray or black stains. It's doubtful that anyone would clean up after the fire without attending to the chimney system itself, but anything is possible.

If a homeowner is really neglectful, he or she may have operated the chimney after the fire occurred. If this happened, there will be other signs to watch out for.

One is pieces of cracked flue lining on the firebox floor. A masonry chimney expands and contracts as it heats and cools, causing pieces loosened by a chimney fire to fall. Should they get lodged in the system, fallen pieces can also cause backsmoking.

Another is crumbling masonry. While this hazard can be blamed on a few things, the cause is most likely flue gases, which are normally contained by the flue lining. When the chimney heats up, the cracks in the flue expand and gases seep to the chimney walls. The gases, being acidic, attack the masonry, causing damage to the structure. (Another hazardous by-product is the carbon monoxide that can also find its way into your home through these cracks.)

So say you notice some of these flue hazards, and you aren't just visiting or renting—the ink has just dried on the deed. You get to put in a new flue. The good news is that flues, once done right, will serve your grandchildren and just about any heating device they might want to use. The bad news is that after you put one in, you won't be able to afford to buy anything else (a new flue runs upward of $2,000).

So how does one shop for a new flue? Flues come in all shapes and sizes and forms. Some come in bags (a poured-in-place liner that is basically a masonry mixture dumped into the chimney and then glazed for protection), some come in pre-made tubes that are dropped into the chimney, filled in with insulator and vibrated into place.

Whatever option you choose, be sure that the flue has been safety-tested and listed by the Underwriters Laboratories Inc. to UL1777 (2100°) and that the listing includes installations in masonry chimneys with Zero-Clearance to combustible materials. What this means is that the flue will be able to withstand the high temperatures and damaging acids and moisture associated with woodburning. The flue will also withstand the different requirements of just about any woodburning appliance you might throw at it or, in this case, throw up it.

WATER DAMAGE

Another major problem for flues and chimneys is water damage.

Since a masonry chimney is made up of a variety of materials including brick, mortar, concrete, concrete block, stone, flue tile, steel, and cast iron, water damage can be a big problem.

All masonry chimney construction materials, except stone (which needs lots of mortar to bind it together so you might as well worry about it, too), will suffer accelerated deterioration if they have too much water contact. Should water find its way into the masonry, the constant freeze/thaw process (imagine how many times that occurs when you are lighting fires during the winter) can cause materials to expand and crumble.

Water also does things like rust the damper; deteriorate metal fireboxes; rust the fireplace accessories and doors; rot any adjacent wood; waterstain your wallpaper, walls, and ceilings; clog the clean doors; stain the chimney exterior; decay the exterior mortar; crack your flue lining; collapse the hearth support; and occasionally tilt or collapse your chimney. And it makes fires harder to start, and smells moldy, too.

Your best line of defense—and, for once, a cheap one, too!—is a chimney cap or rain cover, as it is called. These caps are so good at keeping the water out that the UL specifies that any chimney lining system that is approved by them must include a chimney cap. Since the average chimney flue opens up to be about 13″ × 13″, you can imagine how much snow and rain finds its way down your hatch.

A chimney cap should be easily removable, too, so your sweep can inspect and clean it. Of course it should be made of a sturdy, durable, and corrosion-resistant material. Caps come in a variety of styles—a dome-shaped steel cap, a flat plate of stone or steel, or even better, one of the new ceramic chimney caps copied from European homes—and can be designed to cover a single flue, multiple flues, or the entire chimney top. A full chimney cap can get expensive, but it does protect the whole chimney crown.

🌿

BIRDS AND OTHER ANIMALS It's a cold, cruel world for suburban wildlife and, unfortunately, many take refuge in chimneys. Squirrels, birds, and raccoons are just as damaging to the structure of the chimney as they are cute to look at: Nesting materials can cause serious safety hazards. Animal droppings that fall down the chimney also pose serious health risks, as their diseases can be transmitted to humans. Wire grids and chimney caps can prevent this. If nesting materials and animal droppings have been a problem in the past, it's only a matter of time before they appear again. Sweeps can recommend the best type of protection against unwanted chimney critters.

REPAIRING AND REPLACING CHIMNEY CROWNS

The chimney crown (or chimney wash) tops off the chimney. It covers and seals the chimney from the flue liners to the chimney edge. Because most chimney crowns were originally built with the same mortar that was used in laying the chimney brick, crowns usually aren't able to withstand years of weather abuse without chipping, cracking, or falling apart. If you notice yours is in less-than-perfect condition, it needs to be replaced.

A proper chimney crown should be constructed of a Portland-cement–based mixture and cast so it provides an overhang of about 2″ or more on all sides. The flue liners should project above the chimney edge a minimum of 2″ as well. To keep water from eating at the sides of your chimney, the crown should also have a downward slope (water will spill over the drip edge and not puddle at the base of the chimney).

If the crown is bad enough to need replacing, the chimney mortar joints are probably going to need to be replaced as well. Deteriorated mortar joints are easy targets for water entry. Check to see that yours don't have any gaps or missing mortar and are struck (shaped) in a way that directs water out of the joint. Unfortunately, chimneys in older homes are usually about as watertight as the Titanic. Welcome to the world of pointing.

Pointing (or tuckpointing or repointing) is the technical name for repairing eroded material with new mortar to keep it strong and watertight. The process involves chipping out the loose stuff to a minimum depth of about ¾", brushing the joint clean, and mixing and pressing in new mortar. Then you shape the joint with a special tool to match the original brickwork.

Pointing itself is fairly easy, even somewhat amusing. The hard part is color-matching it to the old brick and doing it all while perched 30 feet in the air on a 40° slope. New mortar often doesn't blend with old, making your chimney look like a bad patchwork dress from the 70s. Masons often mix color tints into their mortars to try matching the old color more closely—which is not easy, since mortar tends to lighten as it cures.

You also have to select the proper hardness for your mortar. A mortar harder than the brick itself will eventually exert pressure that will cause your brick faces to chip and flake. Many restored brick structures have been ruined this way. Best to stick to Type N (one part Portland cement, one part Type S lime, about five parts masonry sand) or Type O (one part Portland, two parts lime, and about seven parts sand).

If you are going to try doing this yourself, read up on repairing brick mortar for basic techniques, and good luck. If, as we do, you own a historic building, seek out a mason, preferably one who is proficient in matching mortars. And don't put it off. Chimneys are the first areas of brickwork to go, and with each passing year (and constant freezing and thawing), the situation gets measurably—and visibly—worse.

Preventing water damage: flashing, counter-flashing, and crickets Flashing is basically the seal between the roofing material and the chimney. Flashing keeps the rainwater and the snow melt from turning your chimney into the Colorado River Basin. In most cases, flashing is a single L-shaped sheet of metal that is attached to the side of the chimney and the roof.

To make your flashing more effective, to guard against getting water damage on your ceiling, wall, or paneling, and to avoid rotting out your rafters and joists, it's best to add counter-flashing. The counter-flashing should overlap the base flashing and be imbedded and sealed in your chimney's masonry joints. This two-element flashing allows both the roof and the chimney to expand and contract at their own rates without breaking the waterproof seal in either area.

If your chimney happens to be located on the low side of the roof, where the flow of runoff is directed against the chimney, it's best to put in a cricket. A cricket is a water deflector that directs water away from the chimney. Crickets should be used mostly on chimneys more than thirty inches wide and are a necessity on step roofs. Crickets look like metal pyramids with a flush side and aren't too awful to install, but you may want to farm this project out as well.

Once you've restored your water-wasted chimney back to good health, it's best to take protective measures to ensure that the whole mess doesn't happen again. Like good shoes, chimneys should be waterproofed.

Most masonry materials are porous and will take in large amounts of water. Common brick is like a sponge and it will not only absorb moisture but wick it to the chimney interior (defective joints and improper mortar or brick only worsen the situation). Several products have been developed especially for chimney waterproofing. These formulas are vapor-permeable, meaning that they allow the chimney to breathe out but not in. Water that has penetrated the chimney is allowed to escape while the waterproofing agent prevents water from entering in from the outside. The up side is that waterproofing can save you a lot of headaches and doesn't cost much. The down side is that it usually lasts only about five to ten years.

If you do have damage, be sure to repair it before waterproofing (the chimney exterior may have to be cleaned, too.) And even though Sarah's two-year-old loves to draw his chimneys purple, never ever try to waterproof using paint—it will only trap moisture inside the chimney.

CLEANING: HOW TO KEEP YOUR CHIMNEY ON THE STRAIGHT AND NARROW

When our cars require servicing, they'll remind us by doing things like stalling in the middle of the freeway and not starting on the morning of the big meeting. A chimney will never do anything that obvious to tell us it needs servicing, but the result of not properly caring for your chimney can be far more disastrous—dirty chimneys were cited as the cause of 28% of fires in 1988—the most recent statistic as of this writing—with property loss estimated at $56.6 million.

Every time a fire is built in your fireplace—whether it be with wood, manufactured logs, or even gas logs—combustion products are released, and sent up the chimney into the atmosphere. Other by-products like soot and creosote cling to the side of the chimney, where they can catch fire as sparks drift up.

One good way to avoid these pesky deposits, and thus chimney fires, is to be sure your fires always burn hot. Unfortunately, complete combustion—which happens when all the products are eliminated, somewhat like when your oven self-cleans—occurs at higher temperatures than most fires and chimneys will allow. Hence the need to have your chimney cleaned.

The good news is that unless you're handy with a broom twice your size and are able to sweep on steep slopes, no one expects you to clean your own chimney. Your local chimney sweep is actually eager to do this for you. Please note that these are serious professionals doing a serious and necessary job and you should be no less discriminating when choosing someone to clean your chimney than you are when choosing a mechanic for your car.

While chimneys may appear to be fairly simple constructions when compared to the rest of the house, as this chapter testifies, a lot can go wrong up there. Any good chimney sweep will not only clean your chimney but inspect it. This is something you should also be doing yourself every few months. And should your chimney yield any of these potentially dangerous but very solvable problems, be sure to contact your chimney sweep immediately.

Finding a good and honest chimney sweep is thankfully somewhat easier than finding a good and honest mechanic. Consult your local yellow pages and check the advertisements for a chimney sweep who has been certified by the National Chimney Sweep Guild (NCSG), the national not-for-profit organization that regulates the industry. While no official nod from any organization is a guarantee, these men and women have passed strict exams that ensure their knowledge of national codes, clearances, standards, and practices. Certified chimney sweeps also know your local and state codes backward and forward. While most certified chimney sweeps have insurance, be sure to check that it's current and that their record with the Better Business Bureau is spotless.

How many times a year your chimney should be swept is a tricky question. If you burn often, a cleaning in spring and a cleaning at about New Year's is in order. If you burn only occasionally, you can get away with one yearly cleaning after the burning season. If you burn wood only a few times a year (holiday burners, as they say), you might be able to squeak by with less frequent cleanings if you are diligent about your own home inspections.

Every visit should start with a thorough inspection. The sweep should then clean the chimney and rid the works of any debris. At the end of the visit, be sure to get a complete written report of the chimney sweep's findings. In most states, chimney sweeps do not have the right to "red tag" or condemn a chimney as unsafe but may tell you if they feel your chimney should not be used.

If a problem is found, the written report should clearly state the cause of the problem, the risk to the system, and what will be required to fix it. As with any service, no work should be done without your consent. You should look over the report with the chimney sweep and sign it upon your satisfaction. Should any serious problems arise with the chimney, this signed report will be your proof to the insurance company that you properly maintained the chimney.

Even better is the modern technology now utilized by some sweeps: Video cameras are dropped down the flue, and they can focus in on specific problems. Videotaping trouble zones is usually free when the sweep needs to show a homeowner the damage done and it can indeed save money, as many hard-to-reach areas have had to be physically pulled apart in the past. This way the camera does the dirty work and you can effortlessly climb down the chimney with the sweep to have a look. Many sweeps even offer a taping of an inspected chimney (the highest estimate we found was $50)—a useful item for your home-video library should you have the kind of insurance company that might someday come up with the notion that you were to blame for the chimney fire that damaged your property. Videotape makes for a pretty convincing case when backed up with a signed, written report.

3

LIGHTING THE
COUNTRY FIRE

There are as many ways to light a fire as there are ways to make a cake. Most of us first learned to make a fire as a Boy or Girl Scout and stayed with that method. Others have tried variations like the tepee or crow's nest. And others of us, well, others of us toss it all in there and pray it lights. Here is a more concise way to do it.

THE BASICS

Most fires are started with three basic elements: tinder, kindling, and firewood.

Tinder, loosely defined, is something with a low flash point that will light instantly. Most people use three or four pieces of newspaper that have been wadded into a ball but some devotees insist on rolling theirs into logs or twisting them into sticks. We tried all these different methods and found the plain old wadded paper seemed to do the best (rolled logs burn too much at the ends and sticks tend to flicker out.) Experts warn against using colored paper as tinder, since the chemicals used in the dyes can be noxious when burned.

Kindling is usually tiny splits of soft wood that will burn hot and long enough that the logs themselves will catch. Be sure that the kindling is super dry and sufficient to last about fifteen minutes. If you are a junkie for good smells, as we are, try some pine or tiny applewood branches. Just as a word of caution, though, there is nothing that goes up faster than dried-out Christmas tree branches. Overloaded kindling in a cold chimney can turn on you quickly and leap out. While you don't want to skimp (it's the only fuel that will produce heat and ignite the larger pieces), use your head and be sure that the elements in your kindling will take more than ten seconds to combust completely.

One technique that has gained popularity in recent years is to use fatwood as kindling. Most fatwood is just pieces of the stumps of pine trees. The stumps, over time, become steeped in resin (pitch), so they light easily and burn well. Fatwood is certainly not the cheapest kindling on the block but if you enjoy using products that make your life somewhat easier, this is one (it makes a nice gift, too).

If you do purchase fatwood, look for products that come from developing countries. Honduras, for example, has started a program that allows Indios and locals to go to the lumber mills and hack the useless stumps into fatwood. CODEFOR, the government-controlled timber management bureau, claims to plant three trees for every one of these stumps that it removes. Fatwood from Honduras is supposed to bring much-needed money into the households of these workers and speed up reforestation while creating a second-use product. We have seen documentation from the American embassy verifying these claims about fatwood and feel comfortable at this point in recommending it to our readers who want an environmentally sound product to use.

Firewood is the last basic needed for a successful fire. We have covered firewood at length but want to stress the importance of being sure that the wood is dry and split into a size that won't overload your fireplace (using wood that is too bulky or odd-shaped will choke the fire and may even roll out as the tinder and kindling shift).

Once you have the basics on hand, you need only two more elements—fire and oxygen.

Taking a match to paper is the most conventional way to light your fire. Fireplace matches are certainly nice to have but are hardly a necessity. If you need even more convenience, there are a few options. Some people still utilize a firestone or fireball, which is basically a piece of clay soaked in kerosene. You place the stone in the fireplace, light it, and remove it once the fire gets going. When not in use, the stone sits in its cast-iron pot (after it has cooled from the fire, of course, unless you want a Molotov cocktail in your living room). Some people (like the manufacturers) insist that these are safe, but you can pretty much forget them if you have kids around or don't really treasure the idea of digging around in your fire.

Other options are firelighting gel packets or bricks. With gel packets, you simply place one on top of the stacked wood and light an edge. Bricks, usually mixtures of sawdust, wax, and kerosene, are placed on the bottom of the stacked wood and light an edge. These commercial preparations that guarantee a light are again helpful if you can't seem to light paper, but they really add up if you are anything other than an occasional burner.

The option that makes the most sense for people who have trouble lighting fires but enjoy one at the end of the day, are gas lighters. This is probably the best fireplace toy to come around in some years. Different from a gas fireplace, these starter mechanisms are basically gas burners that run in a line under your andirons. When you're ready to burn, you just toss on some kindling and logs, and turn a valve to start the thing going. The flame then flicks on and lights everything up. Once the fire is established, you just turn the valve again and the burner shuts off. Perfect for older people, these burners make lighting a fire an easy task and guarantee sure-fire results—pardon the pun. The only drawback is having an exposed pipe prominently displayed on your firebox floor, but we've found that you can bury the pipe quite nicely under a layer of ash.

We don't have to tell you this, we're sure, but it bears repeating: Never ever add any sort of fuel or gasoline to a fire to get it going (not even charcoal lighter fluid, which is meant for outdoor fires).

Oxygen is the final key to a successful fire. Most of it comes in the form of the draft that you get by opening the damper, the object that acts as a door to open and close the passageway to the flue.

So now you have all the things you need for a proper fire—tinder, kindling, firewood, a way to light it, and the oxygen to fan the flames. But how do you make all these things work together?

As we said before, there are lots of ways to make a fire. After considerable trial and error, we've found the following to be the best way.

Always begin by making sure your damper's open, then see that you have a bed of ashes at least two inches thick. Bank a heavier layer against the back to reflect heat into the room and provide a bed for the new coals to drop on. To get the most warmth, plan on laying the fire as close to the edge of the andirons as possible without endangering anything.

Start by placing two medium pieces of firewood across the andirons (if you don't have any andirons, two pieces of wood can be

To build a good fire, start by placing two pieces of medium wood across the andirons, put three or four well-wadded pieces of paper between them, add five or six pieces of kindling on top, and light away.

placed perpendicular to the hearth to serve in their place). Put three or four well-wadded pieces of paper between them and add five or six pieces of kindling (a ½–¾″ diameter) on top. If someone has cleared out all the ashes, loosely bunch a few pieces of newspaper and shove them underneath the whole thing (but don't use paper if you are lighting the fire with anything other than a match).

Next, light away. We like to hit all the end points of the paper and the kindling. Long matches will save the tips of your fingers and are fun to use but the kitchen kind and even the cigarette kind will work in a pinch. Try not to use a lighter; we have been desperate and resorted to that a few times, we confess, but exposing the fluid to a possible flame or spark is hazardous.

Once the thing is starting to light, stand back and wait. The biggest mistake in fire-lighting is rushing the process. It takes at least fifteen minutes for a fire to start to roar. Once it does start to go, add two larger pieces of wood lying opposite to the way of the ones you started with. If you want a long-burning fire, put a large log against the back grate and keep one or two smaller logs in front of it. The back log reflects heat up to the forward logs and, because it takes longer to burn, keeps the fire steady.

So let's say that you just did all this and you're looking at pile of smoking logs and no fire. First check that you left sufficient room (see illustration) for the oxygen to get to the firewood. Next be sure that you didn't overload the fire. If you did, take the larger logs out of the fire, add more kindling and a few pieces of paper, and light it again.

But let's say the fire seems not to be drawing, either. You've got to start over by preheating the chimney. When the damper to your chimney is closed, the temperature in your chimney is similar to the temperature outside. The house, hopefully, is much warmer. To help balance this equation, you need to preheat, or else the cold air coming down will force the smoke from the fire back into the house.

To preheat, once you have your fire built but before you light it, take a piece of newspaper, roll it up, and light the end. Once it's lit, carefully hold the paper above the fire you have laid, reaching up into the chimney. (It's best not to try this while wearing your favorite white cashmere sweater.) This will help draw the initial smoke up the chimney. To get this technique to work, you may have to repeat it a few times, depending on the temperature and the height of the chimney.

Once your fire has burned a bit, you'll want to shift things around to keep the fire even. (Our friends, the Monahans, call this "nagging the fire," as the process involves periodic small, stabbing movements.) Remember that logs burn because of their proximity to other logs. Fires start and burn most vigorously between pieces of wood—as the heat from one piece of wood contributes to heating the second and vice versa. So don't space the logs too far apart when shifting them. Don't pack them too tightly or they will be unable to breathe and the flame will die out; but do be sure to keep them close enough for contact.

While you're nagging the fire, take a few more minutes to spread the coals evenly. What you are shooting for here is an even thick-

🌿

SETTING YOURSELF UP FOR A CLEANER-BURNING FIRE? There has been talk of using a new fire-building technique to produce a cleaner-burning fire. While we haven't seen any test results that support this claim, we thought we'd pass it on so you could add it to your fireplace repertoire.

🌿

As Boy Scouts and Girl Scouts, we learned how to make a campfire: a couple of small logs on the bottom with newspaper and kindling stacked between them, then larger logs on top. This new way is basically the same thing...only built upside-down. Start with large logs criss-crossed on the bottom, smaller logs on top of that, and then finish the whole thing off with kindling and newspaper. In conventional fires, the larger pieces of firewood heat up and they release some gases that escape through the chimney. With this new technique, the gases ignite as they pass upward through the flame, thereby producing a "cleaner"-burning fire.

The traditional, "Girl Scout" method

The "new" method

ness, distributed nicely under the areas that are being burned. People who create picture-perfect-looking fires for a living do this so that flames lap over each log (yes, magazine, movie, and TV advertisers pay these stylists to do this, though gas is quickly putting them out of business). Even if you don't anticipate *House Beautiful*'s dropping by, do it to avoid the hot spots that burn your fire at one end and leave the other to smolder itself out.

EXTINGUISHING THE FIRE

All good things must come to an end and that includes fires. Often, though, your firelight leisure comes to an end before your fire does and you have to make sure that it's safe to leave. The best way to do this is to take any substantial logs that are unburned and stand them on their ends at the back of the firebox. Make sure that they cannot topple over (of if they do, that they simply fall harmlessly behind the grate) and cover any live coals with a heavy layer of ash. If you have doors, just shut them. If you only use a damper, be sure that nothing is still smoking before you shut it down for the night.

Should you plan to start a fire again in the morning, or later on, you can use a technique called banking. Banking allows you to use a fire over and over without using kindling and paper again. To do this, you simply push the hot coals towards the back and bury them under a light layer of ash. The next morning you just rake out the coals and throw on more wood—with no need to start from scratch. Be sure to take out any wood that could ignite and toss it to the side. (Wait about ten minutes for the logs to cool down and then place them in something fireproof like a metal bucket and sit them outside.) Using this technique, coals can stay in this semidormant state for about two days.

4

THE SAFE FIREPLACE:

Chimney fires, kids, indoor pollution, and ashes

CHIMNEY FIRES

L et's say you got your chimney cleaned in the way we told you to. You never use a fuel mix that will overpower your chimney's temperature limits. There's no reason to expect that you'll ever be faced with a chimney fire, right? Wrong. Even the best-laid fires can become chimney infernos. It's no coincidence that over twenty percent of house fires are caused by woodburning appliances.

What causes chimney fires? Well, you know from Chapter Two that creosote is the major culprit here. While it looks as innocent as tar-colored, day-old oatmeal, beware. All it takes is the right combination of oxygen and heat and you'll have a serious house fire to contend with.

Again, here are a few more precautions against chimney fires. One, when you build a fire, get a good blaze going for about half an hour. This should heat all the surfaces of the chimney and vaporize some of that nasty creosote. Second, use well-seasoned wood—this is just another of the 1,001 reasons why it's better than "green" wood. Third, never overfuel a fire by adding more than three logs at a time. And fourth, when cousin Fred is tending the fire, don't ever let him add one of those Duraflame logs. (If you must use them, never light up more than one at a time.)

WHAT TO DO IN CASE OF A CHIMNEY FIRE

So you're taking care of the chimney, following the precautions, and one day when you are starting or refueling your fire, you suddenly begin to hear cracking sounds. Not the happy snaps, crackles, and pops of a hearty blaze, but a sinister cracking sound that seems as though it could break your house in two. You'll know it when you hear it because it's usually followed by a sound that can only be likened to standing under a 747.

The second you suspect a chimney fire, do these three things immediately: First, close the damper, if you can—this will cut off the oxygen supply and begin to subdue and suffocate the fire. Second, alert everyone in the house that they must be prepared to evacuate. (Be sure to reconfirm your safe meeting point so you'll be able to do an instant head count.) Third, alert the fire department—while you may be able to control this yourself, you won't want to have to wait for the pros if you find out you can't.

Your chimney is now trying to withstand heat of up to 2,500° Fahrenheit. Chances are your chimney will begin to crack and blow out gaps. In the worst case, flames and sparks might be shooting out of the chimney onto the roof or into trees. (If you have the presence of mind, send someone out to check for you.) If sparks are shooting out and you haven't already summoned the fire department, do so on the double and evacuate everyone but yourself. You have a last line of defense here unless the fire's spread to the adjacent walls and roof. If it has, grab any photo albums within reach and get out.

Assuming the fire has contented itself to rage only in your chimney, make sure your damper and ducts are closed. Next, grab a fire extinguisher and douse the original fire. If you haven't already purchased a dry-chemical pressurized canister extinguisher for your woodbox, do so today. As a matter of fact, you should have one handy in every room with any fire hazards, which, if you're like us, includes the kitchen and garage. Make sure every adult in the house knows how to use it. (This is also a good time to remind you to put a smoke alarm in every room and check the batteries frequently. Even though you never leave a fireplace unattended while it's burning, a smoke alarm may save your life someday.)

NEVER EVER TRY TO PUT OUT A FIRE WITH WATER UNLESS IT'S YOUR ONLY AND FINAL CHOICE. Water and steam will spread the hot particles over a wider area. And if that doesn't do your house in, the cold water douse will crack the metal parts of your chimney and the floor. But if it's between that and nothing, use the water.

THE AFTERMATH

If your firefighting has been effective, it's time to inspect the damage. First, and most importantly, never open the damper or any draft controls. The creosote that most likely started this disaster can smolder for hours and you might just awaken the beast again. Your system has been severely damaged and should be inspected only by professionals. There is a popular myth that the raging blaze that could have engulfed your entire house does a really good sweep job instead. Don't believe this for a minute and don't even contemplate starting another fire until someone gives you the a-ok. The firefighters you summoned should be able to do this for you and your chimney sweep will probably be able to make any needed repairs.

SPECIAL CONSIDERATIONS FOR CHILDREN

Kids have been told not to play with fire probably since the first cave mother watched in amazement as two sticks ignited. Then why, in this modern day, are preschoolers twice as likely as any other age group to die in a fire? We don't want our kids, your kids, or anyone's kids becoming the next statistic so take a few minutes each month to hold family fire drills and to remind children of the importance of safety around the fireplace. Please.

Children should know that matches and lighters are tools, not toys, and that only adults should use them. Keep matches stored away and out of reach. Tell your preschoolers to get an adult immediately if they even see matches or lighters and not to touch them. All children should understand that matches and lighters only have one use and that misusing them can be fatal. Nothing beats warming yourself by a glowing fire after a day of sledding or iceskating, but warn your children against resting too close to the fire. Keep at least 36″ between the screen and your child. Fireplaces are not playscapes and kids should be discouraged from horsing around near them—a stray shirttail takes no time to catch fire. Sitting by the fire should be a safe, quiet family pastime. Be extra careful with glass doors. While they offer more protection, the glass and trim get hot in a hurry and can inflict some nasty burns.

Children should also never be allowed to throw things into the fire. While many of us adults get a wicked pleasure out of watching unpaid bills and photos of old lovers go up in smoke, children can be seriously injured by the intense heat and sparks created from burning materials other than wood.

It goes without saying that the whole family should be ready in case of an emergency. Should clothing accidentally catch, it's important to be familiar with the simple **Stop** (stay where you are), **Drop** (drop to the ground), and **Roll** (cover your face with your hands to protect it and roll over and over until the flames are extinguished) technique. It can save your life.

Everyone in the house should also know the fire escape route for every room, with at least two options in case smoke or flames blocks one exit. Pick a safe spot away from the house for everyone to meet so you can determine if anyone is still inside. As children have a tendency to hide from fire—toddlers are often tragically found dead under beds and in closets—they must know to "get out and stay out."

And always be sure to practice crawling on the floor, since the cleanest air is found several inches off the ground. An easy way to learn is to hold a blanket, representing smoke, about two feet over the children's head and get them used to shimmying under it to safety.

To encourage safe habits, allow your children to assist you in making the fire by asking them to help you select the logs or collecting twigs for kindling. Fires are a reminder of the warmth and safety of the home. Let them stay that way.

INDOOR AIR POLLUTION

When it happened, she thought that the wine had given her a headache. They'd been sitting in front of the fire all night, having dinner. The only light for their Valentine's eve supper had been candlelight and the glow of the fire. But by the time dessert rolled around, our friend Lynn was dizzy enough to beg off the rest of her romantic evening for a quick trip to the emergency room—this wasn't the pleasant champagne buzz she normally got, this wasn't even an early onset of vertigo. The doctor told her some hours later she was probably poisoned by the combustion pollutants that were being emitted from her fireplace.

Lynn told us that she couldn't believe it. She'd moved to Boulder from New York City to escape a polluted atmosphere and ended up being made sick by the air in her own home. Face it—the prospect of indoor pollution is scary stuff.

But how likely is this to happen? And how does it happen?

We have a lot of air-needy items in our homes: the furnace, the water heater, the clothes dryer, the bathroom fan, the exhaust fan over the stove, and, oh yes, we human beings. With such a big demand, you'd assume your house must have a sophisticated air-intake system. Well, it probably doesn't.

Most homes were once built with enough cracks and gaps that fresh air used to flow through them quite regularly. But then we all got wise to conserving energy and we insulated, caulked, and weatherstripped every nook and cranny and replaced old, leaky windows and exterior doors. And in the process, we made our houses so airtight that we forgot to let a little in to breathe with.

It's this lack of fresh-air exchange that is at the root of indoor air pollution. What happens is that our combustion appliances—those that require fuel and air for cooking or heating—don't end up venting properly because they lack an escape route for their exhaust and instead release their pollutants into the home.

Bear in mind that combustion appliances are usually safe. But under certain conditions, combustion appliances such as fireplaces and woodstoves can damage your health or even kill you. Possible health effects range from headaches, dizziness, sleepiness, and watery eyes to breathing difficulties. Now we know this sounds a bit alarmist but you should take indoor air pollutants seriously—studies have shown that the air in our homes can be even more polluted than the outdoor air in big cities.

So what is in this deadly air? The most hazardous pollutant is carbon monoxide. Each year more than 200 people die of combustion-appliance-related carbon monoxide poisoning. (Exposure to carbon monoxide reduces the blood's ability to carry oxygen.) The frightening thing is that carbon monoxide is odorless, colorless, and almost impossible to detect. Breathing carbon monoxide at low levels can cause fatigue and increase chest pain in people with chronic heart disease, it can give the rest of us nasty headaches, dizziness, and weakness, and it can cause sleepiness, nausea, vomiting, confusion, and disorientation. At very high levels, carbon monoxide can cause loss of consciousness and death.

And that's not even the only pollutant produced from burning fuels. Some other goodies are nitrogen dioxide, particles (which can have hazardous chemicals attached to them) and sulfur dioxide. Symptoms of these poisons are as follows:

Nitrogen dioxide—breathing high levels can cause irritation of the respiratory tract and shortness of breath.

Particles—exposure to these suspended in the air can cause eye, nose, throat, and lung irritation. Particles can bring on symptoms of respiratory distress, especially in people with chronic lung disease or heart problems.

Sulfur dioxide—exposure at low levels can cause eye, nose, and respiratory-tract irritation. At high levels, the lung airways narrow, causing wheezing, chest tightness, or breathing problems.

So if this stuff is undetectable, how do you protect yourself? First, check for clues. Some indicators of possible spillage into your home are persistently stuffy, stale, or smelly air, very high humidity, often showing up as moisture on windows (which also encourages biological pollutants such as dust mites, molds, and bacteria), and accumulations of soot around the fireplace.

Should any of these factors be present, be sure to ask your chimney sweep for possible backdrafting. We've discussed backdrafting and what to do about it at length in this book. Ironically, air-poisoning most often occurs not when backdrafting is an obvious problem but when a fire is calmly dying in the hearth. How? A dying fire allows the chimney to cool and reduce its draw. Normal demand for inside air may cause a downdraft, spilling dangerous fumes into the house and into the living space. Reason number 103 for airtight glass doors.

You can also take preventive measures against indoor air pollution. Start by making sure that you select the right heating appliances for your home.

First, always choose vented appliances that have separate vents whenever possible. Second, buy only those combustion appliances that have been tested by our two favorite (and most respected) testing laboratories, the Underwriters Laboratories (UL) and the American Gas Association (AGA.) Third, make sure the appliance is the correct size for the area you want to heat (if the unit is new, your builder can tell you this, or you can contact the manufacturer). And finally, if you are buying a new woodstove, make sure it's EPA-certified so that the amount of pollutants you and Mother Nature are exposed to are, at worst, limited.

Next, see that the appliance has been properly installed. Professionals should follow the installation instructions to the letter as well as comply with local codes. Improperly installed appliances can release dangerous pollutants into your home from day one and create a potential fire hazard. Be sure that your installer also checks for backdrafting on all your appliances.

Also make sure that your house has adequate ventilation. To guard against indoor air pollution, be sure that the house has an adequate supply of fresh air. If you are truly curious about the specifics of your house's air flow or just want to figure out how energy-efficient your house is, you can invest $150 or so in a blower door test. This test measures your home's air changes and should help you locate massive air leaks should you want to regulate the air flow without starving the house of air.

And of course be sure to have your fireplace and woodstove inspected frequently and maintained.

If these measures don't make you feel awfully secure about the possibility of air poisoning (or if you have someone in the house with chronic heart disease or respiratory problems), you may want to pick up a carbon monoxide detector called the "Quantum Eye." This device, rather cheap for the piece of mind and protection it offers, costs about $12.95 and is available at many hardware stores or by mail from the Quantum Group (Dept. FH, 1211 Sorrento Valley Road, Suite D, San Diego, CA 92121; 619/457-3048).

ASHES TO ASHES, DUST TO DUST

Ashes are a lot like a stale love affair—after the spark has gone out, it's time to clean out our hearth and dispose of the evidence. So what to do with all that gray matter? First make sure that there is not even one hot speck of ash left. No tepid coals, no glowing chunks of wood leftovers, no nothing. They shouldn't even be warm if you can help it. This stuff is not innocent dust lingering here—don't treat it as such.

Once you're sure your ashes have cooled, get the little shovel and broom that have been sitting looking so pristine next to those warhorses in your fireplace tool caddy. You should also have a metal bucket handy. (We use our ash buckets to hold scented pinecones in off-duty hours.) Taking care to work slowly and with a steady hand, transfer the ashes to the bucket. As tempting as it is to scoop it out in great gobs, don't—this stuff flies. As the Grateful Dead once so rightly sang, "ashes to ashes, all fall down." And they do. On your carpet, your sweater, your nice wood floor. (If you do manage to dump some, don't run for dampened paper towels. Scoop up as much as you can using two edges, then dab up the rest with a dry rag.)

   ❧   TO CLEAN THE FLOOR OF YOUR FIREBOX, *use half a cup of washing soda mixed with two gallons of warm water. Wear gloves and allow the floor to dry out completely before lighting any fires. Use the mixture as sparingly as possible, since getting the floor wet can reduce heat output.*

LIGHT THE COUNTRY FIRE

And for God's sake, don't do what our neighbor did one Christmas after receiving one of those green-canister clean machines, that is, try to vacuum out your fireplace. The upholstery cleaner in town still gets a big chuckle out of that one.

Once you've gotten all the ashes in the bucket, put a lid on it and transfer them to a plastic or paper bag to be dumped.

But if you've read this far, you know that wood is one of our great renewable resources, and that wood ashes contain minerals—like potash, potassium, phosphorus, iron, silicon, and sulfur among others—all of which are very good for your soil. So sprinkle some in your garden and reap the rewards in better veggies.

Ashes also keep away certain bothersome pests. Slugs and snails, for instance, won't slither across them. (Yes, ashes cling like the devil to them, and they enjoy that about as much as you do.) Root maggots also hate ashes, so sprinkle some around your carrots, onions, beets, and the like after they've grown about six inches. To keep cutworms away from your tomato patch, dig a trench a few inches deep around it, and fill the trench with ashes. And bark-borers will be repelled if you spread a layer of ashes around your young fruit trees.

Should a green thumb elude you, ashes have lots of other uses. Ashes are as effective as salt for melting snow, and they won't harm your car or your water supply the way salt does.

You can also use it to make alkali, a key ingredient in homemade soap. Trickle purified water through wood ashes and boil down the remains to concentrate it. (Be careful not to use aluminum or cast-iron vessels in this operation, as they can affect the alkalis.)

If you're ambitious enough to make your own soap, perhaps you'll enjoy our final tip. A layer of ashes forms a physical barrier to odor, and the alkalinity of ashes interferes with both bacterial action and the growth of fly larvae—so they are perfect for deodorizing your outhouse.

66

5

A FIRE IN THE BELLY:
Woodstoves

Around the mid 1700s, an American named Ben Franklin got to working on the problem of inefficient fireplaces. (The European nobility was getting a little sick of freezing their corsets off in their drafty stone castles while the peasants remained toasty in their mud-and-wood huts in the sheltered forests.) What Franklin came up with was a freestanding fireplace with an open front and cast-iron sides. The Franklin fireplace, as it was called, made ordinary fireplaces a thing of the past and gave our country the first of what we now know as woodstoves.

Franklin's invention worked this way: The open-front unit fit into a fireplace that had been bricked up except for a passage that led to the chimney, where smoke could escape. But to create more heat and to allow the wood to burn more slowly, Franklin added a damper that could control the flow of air to the flames. There were also upright metal plates that created baffles that allowed the woodburning gases to actually be burned as fuel as well. The baffles also allowed the stove itself to heat up and radiate warmth into the room.

This basic model, with some improvements by others, found its

A basic Franklin stove

way into just about every American home and didn't undergo any serious modifications until about 1970, when America plunged into an
energy crunch. A shortage of fossil fuels drove prices sky high and
many Americans turned back to wood for heating their homes.

Though woodburning helped abate the energy crisis, it created another crisis in its place—an environmental crisis. Scientists discov-
ered that the millions of tons of smoke pouring out of just about
every American house were filled with noxious agents (carbon
monoxide, hydrocarbons, and formaldehyde, to name a few). Soon
the newspapers warned of high pollution readings, and some com-
munities kept school kids home on "bad air" days. Certainly measures had to be taken.

In 1986, Oregon prohibited the sale of the most-polluting stoves.
That same year New York State and the Natural Resources Defense
Council threatened the EPA with a lawsuit if they didn't do some-

thing on a national scale to alleviate the problem. It was then that environmentalists, scientists, and state agencies got together and established standards for new stoves.

THE NEW ERA

To meet Environmental Protection Agency requirements, a stove manufacturer must now send a stove from each of its model lines to one of eight EPA-certified commercial testing laboratories. There the stoves are fired up and the particulate emissions (solid, unburned hydrocarbons) are measured. Additional components of wood smoke are also gauged, but a low particulate emission means that other pollutants are scarce, too. The EPA's benchmark is the number of grams of particulate given off during an hour of burning (g/hr.) Stoves that fail the test cannot be manufactured. (At the end of 1993, 405 models of stoves had been certified.)

The EPA sought to implement these regulations in two phases: The first phase covered stoves made between July 1988 and July 1990. Catalytic stoves made during that period may emit no more than 5.5 g/hr and noncatalytic stoves no more than 8.5 g/hr. The second phase pertained to stoves made after July 1990 and dictated that catalytics can't emit more than 4.1 g/hr and noncatalytic stoves no more than 7.5 g/hr. There was, however, a two-year grace period following each of these deadlines, but even taking that into account, all stoves now on the market should comply with the more stringent Phase II requirements. (The EPA didn't extend these rulings to open fireplaces, wood-fired boilers and furnaces, or wood cookstoves, but it did include fireplace inserts and "airtight" fireplaces with gasketed doors.)

So what exactly are catalytic and noncatalytic stoves? A "catalytic" stove uses a catalyst combuster to cut the emissions, somewhat the way your car's system works. A catalyst combuster is just a ceramic cylinder that has been coated with a metal catalyst (like platinum or palladium). Smoke is made up of combustible gases that will burn up at about 1,000°. Most woodstove fires, however, don't get up over 600°, which means that a lot of pollution and energy go up the chimney. With this catalyst, however, smoke will burn at 500° and less of it will pass up the chimney into the air. The irony of these stoves is that the more smoke you throw at it, the harder the catalyst works and the more heat it kicks out. (Make sure, though, never to throw trash, colored newspaper or painted wood, or just about anything that isn't cordwood at it, since these will ruin your catalyst.)

Some combustors reach 1,600° in normal use, just on the energy provided by the smoke. Put a catalyst combustor in a well-designed stove and it can reduce emissions up to an incredible 90%.

Noncatalytic stoves, on the other hand, are stoves that are not equipped with this combustor. These stoves work by capturing and igniting gases by regulating airflow and forcing the gases over superheated baffles made of steel or masonry. To comply with EPA standards, most noncats have been elevated to what are called airtight models.

Airtights are the souped-up version of what most people remember from their childhood except that manufacturers have reduced the size of the firebox to increase the temperature and cause more of the emissions to be burned. If you're looking into buying a stove of this kind, look for a firebox about the size of 1.8 cubic feet. Any larger and you'll have more emissions; much smaller and you'll be burning toothpicks (though most stoves do fall into the 1.5-cubic-feet range).

There are a few other drawbacks as well: They need frequent feeding and ash removal, all-night burns are pretty much out of the question, overly insulated units can throw more heat up the chimney than into the room, and they rank behind catalytics and pellet stoves in efficiency. In short, if you are planning on heating your house with airtights, you have a lot of considerations. But if you are just going for that cozy glow and some heat, they can be a good choice. (Despite whatever money you may lose in heating inefficiency, good airtight stoves cut wood use by 30%.)

Should you find yourself with an older stove that looks better than it works, it is possible to buy a catalytic add-on. (The device, a little space-age in appearance, is installed in the lower flue and can deliver an efficiency close to that of a pre-built model.) At a cost of only a few hundred dollars, they are a lot cheaper than going out and buying a new airtight (they start at about $700) or even a new EPA-approved woodstove (between $700 and $1,500.)

Most woodstoves today are made from either steel or cast iron. Steel stoves (and some cast-iron ones) give off both radiant heat (the exterior surface of the stove warms the air around it) and convective heat (cool air is drawn into the convective chamber and returned warm). To boost heat distribution, many steel stoves are available with blowers, though most well-designed stoves work fine on their own.

Steel stoves are often recommended for heating more than one adjacent room, since radiant heat will project in straight lines and not sneak out around corners. When you're shopping, make sure the welds and liners are smooth—not spotty—and the corners should be rounded so you aren't constantly nailing your thighs or impaling the kids. The better steel stoves on the market will have some cast-iron parts.

Cast-iron stoves, on the other hand, are slightly nicer to look at and work well in large, open areas where radiant heat can move freely. While slower to heat up than steel stoves, they're also slower to cool—even when few coals remain, the surface will still kick out heat. When you're looking for cast-iron stoves, check the smoothness of the finish. Be wary of chips and bumps on the castings, as they indicate vulnerability and will lead to cracking.

Soapstone stoves are another alternative you might consider. The surface of these stoves is distinctive and really lovely to look at. Soapstone is also one of nature's most heat-absorbent materials. Like cast iron, which is often used to keep the pieces together, soapstone heats up slowly but stays warm for hours. Soapstone stoves are ideal for people who want to heat their homes overnight and keep embers for banking (keeping coals live for use the next day).

People have a hundred different reasons for what stove they pick. We're sure that after thoroughly investigating woodstoves in the showroom, you'll be drawn to one model or another. The one piece

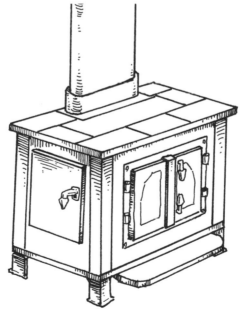

A soapstone stove

of advice that we have is buy the right size stove for the area you wish to heat. Bigger isn't always better. Heat is a good thing but turning your house into a sauna isn't.

LIGHT THE WOODSTOVE FIRE

If you were one of the 750,000 people who purchased a woodstove in the last year, congratulations; you are now one of the millions of people still wrestling with the best way to fire up your trusty new companion.

Let's start off with some common trouble spots: One, wood that isn't properly seasoned. Two, a woodstove that isn't properly installed. Three, your fire-building technique is sabotaging you.

We've devoted a whole chapter to getting the right wood but we'll say it again: Wood should be seasoned to 20% moisture. Unless you get it delivered that way, you'll have to wait at least six months (more in high-humidity areas) for the wood to dry out sufficiently.

To super-dry wood, bring in as much as you have room for and store it near (not too near) your stove. The stove heat will help it surface-dry and the wood will help humidify the air.

If you find that your wood isn't lighting properly, is emitting lots of white smoke, or is not burning completely, you should reread Chapter One or call your dealer for another delivery.

The second problem is a stove that has not been properly installed. Like chimneys, a stovepipe that is either too short or the wrong diameter can sabotage your best-laid fires. And a house that is too airtight can also cause the same problems (again, try cracking a window

To start the woodstove fire, place crumpled newspaper in the woodstove firebox, construct a teepee of kindling surrounding the paper, put a few pieces of medium size wood over the whole thing, open the draft control at the bottom of the stove, open the stovepipe damper, light the newspaper, and presto.

for a short-term fix). If it seems as though improper installation could be your problem (which sometimes happens when folks do it themselves), call your dealer and have him or her check the setup.

Finally, you could be defeating yourself in the way you build your fire. The method that we've found to work best is to start with a couple of sheets of crumpled newspaper, make a tepee of kindling arranged over the paper, and finally place a few medium-sized splits of hardwood in a tepee over the whole thing. Open the draft control at the bottom of the stove and then open the stovepipe damper. Add a match and presto. Once things get going, add hardwood for a long, hot burn.

If you feel the need to cheat, you can use a stick of the fatwood we detailed earlier. You only need one and most likely you'll be able to pass on the newspaper. But again, if you burn fatwood often, this can add up. Some people are fond of squirting deodorized kerosene on their fire to ease lighting. Since this type of kerosene burns as a liquid rather than a vapor, there's not the same danger of explosion. But no fire professional in a million would endorse this kind of shortcut. Best to stick to any of the commercial fire starters if you're this desperate.

Before smoke danger became a big issue, most people would cram the woodstove full and forget it. These days you should tend yours actively. After establishing the coal bed and loading once, you should close the door and dampers but maintain an active airflow, and add fuel frequently rather than loading it to the gills.

We always used to throw the logs that were about to go into the fire on top of the stove for preheating, especially the ones we intended to burn overnight. While we still do that, we never leave the stove unattended for more than a few minutes.

WOODSTOVE MAINTENANCE

Maintaining your woodstove is somewhat similar to maintaining a fireplace. You need to watch for creosote buildup and check that all your pieces are still in one piece.

The most obvious chore is the easiest one—getting the ashes out of the stove. If the stove has no grate, you'll need to use an ash rake. If it does, a shovel will do the job. Put the ashes into a metal pail, as they can remain hot for days after a burn. (You know from the last chapter all the wonderful uses for these ashes.)

As for the stove itself, there are not a lot of things to do to it. A coat of stove-blacking once or twice a year will prevent rust and keep things looking good.

If your stove has thinner-gauge sheet metal, you might also want to check that no spots have experienced a "burn through," which happens when you have a fire too hot for your stove to handle. The metal becomes oxidized and spots thin. Although this doesn't happen often, it's something to be mindful of.

Airtights have door gaskets of asbestos rope. These wear out over time but should be good for ten years. Should you be trying to rehabilitate an older stove, this is one of the first things you'll have to check. (For more info on rehabilitating older stoves, see the Resources section.)

Your stovepipe is more complex. Periodically make sure that all the parts are still connected. If the connections are loose or there is space between the joints, sparks and creosote may escape. Joints and bends should be monitored, as they are especially susceptible.

Stovepipes are very vulnerable to sulfuric acid. This acid, formed from smoke condensation, will corrode the surface over time. Replace immediately any section that starts to show signs of corrosion.

It's also important to inspect your chimney. The procedure for inspecting stove chimneys is essentially the same as for fireplace chimneys (see Chapter Two) and they should be cleaned just as often by a certified chimney sweep.

We heard some country lore about sprinkling salt on your wood fire to reduce the creosote buildup that causes problems. While searching for scientific support, we came across products containing sodium chloride (table salt.) When added to a fire of the proper temperature, these products send chemical fumes up the chimney and turn creosote into flakes that then fall on the fire and burn harmlessly. These products are worth a look if you want an extra measure of protection.

6

GETTING THE MOST HEAT
FROM YOUR FIREPLACE:

Dampers, doors, devices, and inserts

I
n the dark ages, way before we ever had something like me-
chanical heating systems, fireplaces were a big necessity. For
those of us who don't want to be at the mercy of the utility
company, those of us who relish self-sufficient living, and those of us
who have waited a weekend for our repairman to return from Bar-
bados while we cool our heels back in Buffalo, fireplaces are still a
big necessity.

However, fireplaces can be downright inefficient (their energy efficiency is a ghastly 5–10%.) So how do you keep your house's heat
from going up with the smoke? Fortunately, there are a lot of products and techniques to keep the warmth inside where it belongs.

First of all, if you only use your fireplace once in a great while and
then merely for the aesthetic appeal, don't go investing lots of
money; it's not worth it. But if you do use it enough, getting maximum heat and encouraging minimum heat loss makes more than
sense—it could save you hundreds of dollars and add value to your
home.

FLUE DAMPERS

A ll fireplaces should have a flue damper. That's the little lid you open and close to allow the smoke to go up the chimney instead of into your living room—the thing that homeowners remind you to open about a hundred times before you make a fire. Leave it open when you aren't making a fire, however, and you may as well leave the front door open in a blizzard; it's the same thing. No matter how tempting it is to idiot-proof your fireplace and keep the damper open permanently (and we're vacation-rental investors so we know the meaning of this temptation), don't do it—you might as well use twenty-dollar bills for kindling next time. Buy one of those cute needlepoint "The Flue is Closed/The Flue is Open" signs to hang. Anything.

For reasons known only to God, real estate agents, and your chimney sweep, occasionally dampers are left missing and not replaced after cleaning or repairs have been done. Make sure one is installed.

GLASS DOORS

G lass doors serve a variety of functions. First, they make very effective spark guards and are helpful for people who have to constantly combat a smoky fireplace (most come with adjustable air vents that can be used to control your fire). Second, glass doors reduce the amount of heat floating up the chimney when you aren't burning. Third, they greatly cut down the amount of pollutants that may come back into the room as the fire dies.

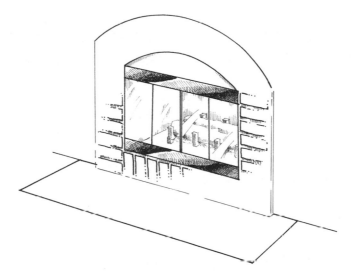

Glass doors—an effective, attractive spark guard

But most people think that all glass doors do is keep heated room air from going up your chimney. Well, yes…and no.

When using glass doors, you have two competing effects—reduced room air loss (which is good) and reduced heat radiation (which is bad).

Tests were done comparing how much heat you get from a fireplace with its glass doors open as opposed to closed. The results showed that glass doors cut the amount of heat radiating back into your room by about 50% and reduce the loss of room air up the chimney by only 20%. By the time you account for the various factors that make glass doors less efficient (leakiness in the joints and panes, the type of glass, the amount of heat generated by the fire as opposed to the amount of heat in the room, etc.), you are probably breaking about even whether you burned with your glass doors entirely open or entirely closed.

Bottom line: Use the doors when you need complete protection against sparks (the mesh kind are more efficient but they do let through some small embers, and one is all you need to sear a nice hole in your rug), when your fire is dying, or when the fireplace is not in use. But for normal woodburning, leave them open.

The good news about getting glass doors is that they can be custom-designed to accommodate just about any fireplace. The bad news is that they aren't cheap. While you have endless design choices and numerous price points, there are only three basic types of glass—tempered, Pyrex, and ceramic. The difference in these three types of glass is not only price but the temperatures they are able to withstand. Tempered glass, the least expensive material, is only good to 700° Fahrenheit before it shatters. Pyrex, by Corning, as anyone who owns bakeware knows, is a little better, good to about 800°. The top of the line, ceramic glass, can heat up to a whopping 1475°.

Do you really need glass fireplace doors that can stand heat double to what your oven could kick out on its best day? Yes and no. The fundamental difference is the shatter point and how comfortable you are with the possibility that your fireplace doors could one day blow out into your living room. Not that this is likely, but it can happen, especially with tempered glass. Tempered glass is just glass that has been sprayed or dipped in a protective coating, and over time—as you repeatedly heat and cool your fireplace—the coating will lose its nice temperament and the glass will shatter eventually.

Ceramic glass, while the most costly, will break only in the case of extreme heat. It will probably not be able to withstand a chimney fire, but it will never shatter. Ceramic glass only breaks. But ceramic glass often won't afford you a clear view of your fireplace (since the glass is wavy and the image of your fire becomes distorted).

A nice compromise is Pyroceram (also a Corning Glass trademark). Not only is Pyroceram less expensive than top-of-the-line ceramic, but it also offers you similar protection and a clear view of your fire. We're not sure if this is a plus or minus, but it has a tinge of amber color.

The only other problem with doors is how often you must clean the glass. Most manufacturers say you can get the creosote (yes, the stuff gets everywhere) off with Windex but we've seen some pretty stubborn stains. A friend of ours solved this problem by rubbing the spots with cool ashes and a soft cloth that had been lightly damp-ened, then buffing with a dry cloth. It really works!

CONVECTION DEVICES

Another way to pump heat back into your home is with convec-tion pipes. (Convection is the rising of hot air and the falling of cold.) You install the pipes in place of your andirons and the logs rest on steel tubes or pipes that loop toward the room. These pipes

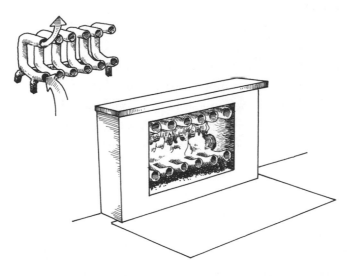

Convection pipes

are heated as the wood burns and the heat moves naturally up the pipes (warm air rises, remember?) and out into your room.

The best models offer a fan that helps move the heat into the room. Some versions have a motor outside the hearth to draw cold air from the room, heat it, then pump it back. Other kinds have a motor beneath the pipes at the bottom of the hearth. Any of these is quite helpful...if a tad noisy.

RADIATION-ENHANCING GRATES

You've probably noticed a lot of strangely shaped racks in fireplace stores. What are they? Radiation grates. These grates replace your andirons and work on the theory that the more you expose heating surfaces to the room, the more heat you get. Their shape permits a more vertical or C-shaped array of wood and directs the heat from the fire and hot coals back into the room as opposed to against the firebox wall.

While these contraptions do help increase heat slightly, they require you to keep a large fire going. They need frequent reloading, since the fuel burns more quickly with the increase in air exposure. The configuration also requires very straight logs and a lot of shifting the fire about, as the top logs burn through quickly (you'll have to reposition a lot of coals). Do the grates make a big difference? Not really. But in a modern room, they really look good.

FIREBACKS

We love the look of a fireback. Many of these old-time heat refractors have beautiful, intricate designs, and can stand on their own as art. Should you ever come across one of these cast-iron beauties at an auction or in a shop, they can add significantly to a room. Do they add heat, though? A small amount, we imagine—there has been no real testing done on the subject—but we love them anyway.

Now for more serious considerations. Please be aware that the following heat options go up in price and, some may feel, down in style, but they also give you an energy efficiency of up to 80%.

You may look at this list and gag. Granted this was not what Ben Franklin had in mind two hundred years ago. Luckily, there are a few options that allow you to keep the integrity of your home's design intact and at the same time boost efficiency.

FIREPLACE INSERTS

A fireplace insert is essentially a woodstove without legs that tucks neatly into your existing structure and utilizes the flue already in place. Most are cast iron but some have glass fronts so you

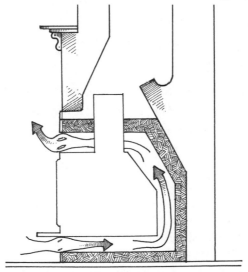

Fireplace insert

don't lose the glow behind doors. With a heat efficiency of up to 60% or more, they can justify their $600 to $1,200 cost.

Inserts work on two principles: They both extract heat and block off some of the room airflow up the chimney.

With the interest in efficiency growing, the range of products is pretty wide. If your chimney and fireplace are interior and exposed, you won't have to worry much about design, as all the heat will be absorbed in the masonry and will ultimately heat the house. If you have an exterior chimney, however, as many of us do, you have to pay attention to what design you buy (you want the least leakage of heat possible), or you'll need to look into insulating your unit with ceramic-fiber insulating board.

You should also pay attention to what kind of doors the unit has. Glass doors, as we know, can be leaky. Cast iron or steel gives a much tighter fit.

Most good inserts come with blowers to insure that the air flow through the heat exchanger is adequate. While they're not always necessary, look for a unit that has one or be sure you know how a blowerless insert will perform for you.

There are, of course, some potential problems when making a change as large as this.

🍂 For a start, your existing chimney may be too big for your insert. Most flues are designed for large, open burning. Inserts don't use as much air, especially when the doors are shut. Flues that are too big mean less draft and increased creosote, both real hazards. The problem can be exacerbated by cool exterior walls in winter—to such a point that the whole system works in reverse, air flows down the chimney, and the smoke pours through the air inlets.

🍂 Inserts also pose a problem when it comes to getting your chimney cleaned. The sweep must either look down the chimney from the roof (which doesn't allow for the fireplace area to be inspected) or the whole thing has to be pulled out. This often means a day of the sweep's time and a hefty tab for you.

🔥 Your chimney also might not be able to handle the increase in temperature. Be sure to have your chimney thoroughly inspected to make sure it can handle the output.

🔥 In some inserts, the combustion gases are vented directly behind the lintel. This spot is normally pretty cool and some wood structures may suddenly catch if the area gets too hot. Be sure to factor this in before anything gets installed.

Finally, even if your flue is in good condition, you'll probably want to have a new one put in for your insert. This is not the cheapest solution to avoiding potential problems, but since a new flue eliminates so many of them, don't be surprised if your installer recommends one. Granted there will be a case when this is not necessary, but most of the time it is (especially with exterior chimneys, which most of us have).

And do have your insert professionally installed. While many of us have gotten handy in ways we never thought possible, expertise goes a long way in insuring safety and performance, which is why you bought the insert to begin with.

FACTORY-BUILT FIREPLACES

Factory-built, prefabricated fireplaces can be divided into two categories: freestanding and built-in. (There is also such a thing as a fireplace furnace that falls into this category but that really isn't the sort of thing most people are considering for their living room.)

Freestanding fireplaces are those units that were considered "decorative" back in the 70s. They are those somewhat egg-shaped fireplaces that sat in the middle of the room, usually painted some kind of "accent" color. They are still being made, and some now come with glass doors. As far as we know, they have no extra efficiency whatsoever over any other totally open fire. But if you need the perfect addition to the playpen couch and lava lamps in your living room, well, this may be for you after all.

Of greater interest to the serious woodburner is the built-in version. Most of these are "zero clearance" fireplaces. What this means, basically, is that the unit is so contained that you can put it next to an interior wood wall, with zero clearance, and not burn the place down.

Since built-in fireplaces can be used in existing constructions as well as new ones, they've gotten pretty popular. You can build around them with any normal materials and end up with something that is pretty normal looking. The differences between built-ins and masonry fireplaces are that prefabs need prefab chimneys (always use the type recommended by the manufacturer), they're light (they can be used on upper stories without damage), and—best of all—they are a lot cheaper ($1,800 to $2,600 fully installed with hearth and mantel; a finished masonry fireplace, by contrast, runs upward of $4,000).

Prefabs can also be really efficient, about 50%. Some models, as with everything else, are better than others. Cheaper models can rust, wear out, and lose their efficiency as a result. When purchasing a prefab, look for a large heat-transfer surface area, a reasonable heat transfer system (again, a blower is your best bet), and airtightness (tight doors and a tight flue damper). If you plan on heating rooms other than the one the fireplace is due to live in, look for a model offering ducting to direct the heat to other rooms.

There is such an animal as a natural-gas fireplace insert as well.

Similar to the woodburning units (except that they have ceramic logs with the closed-combustion chamber), these inserts have efficiencies of up to 75% and can cost up to $2,000 even before installation. As we said in the last chapter, be sure that any gas appliance is certified by the American Gas Association Laboratories with the blue AGA star symbol clearly marked on the appliance.

With these appliances, like the others, you'll have to install a high-temperature flue liner (these units can reach 2,000° or more). Again, size may be an issue. Too small a flue could create emissions resulting from incomplete combustion; too large allows for lingering smoke and creosote buildup.

Needless to say, the options are considerable. There are a lot of products on the market offering a range much wider than we have detailed here. Many manufacturers have added bells and whistles and lots of decorative extras.

If you are truly unsure or want a professional opinion on what would be best—given your design and construction limitations—hire a sweep to come to your house to evaluate things for you (most will do it for $40 to $60). Make sure the technician has a working knowledge of your local codes and has passed the Solid Fuel Safety exam given by the Wood Heat Education and Research Foundation (WHERF).

ALTERNATIVE FUELS:

Gas, propane, and pellets

Imagine coming home after a hard day, plopping down on the couch, hitting a remote control, and presto, instant fire. No logs to haul, no newspaper to crumple. Just a fire burning in the hearth that is almost indistinguishable from a wood fire.

Certainly gas logs have come a long way: Who doesn't remember those awful fake logs with a flame that had all the warmth of a butane lighter? You can now purchase logs that have been painted to look like a variety of woods. Fake ash is available to cover any telltale signs. There are special "coals" that glow with your fire. You can even buy ceramic pinecones and acorns to embellish the look (the fake squirrel sits on the hearth and costs extra). But we digress....

You really can't argue about the convenience of gas. And let's face it, for anyone near a line, gas can save you money. (A study by Mountain Fuel, a Salt Lake City public utility company, cited gas as costing 23 cents an hour to use as opposed to wood, which came in at 88 cents.)

And if your home, along with the majority in America, uses gas fuel, installation is fairly painless—you can update your fireplace or put in a new one without the cost of a traditional woodstove or fire-place insert.

If natural gas isn't an option where you are, you might consider liq-uid petroleum (LP)—propane to us commoners—which is available in most areas. Most manufacturers of gas appliances also offer LP, al-though at a bit higher cost. (But you do get more heat.)

Central to any system are gas burners and refractory cement or ce-ramic logs. This is how the fires are able to look more realistic: First, the appearance of a flickering, golden fire is created by reducing the amount of air entering the firebox. Next, the gas enters the fire-place and is then diffused through sand, vermiculite, or gravel for a natural-looking, irregular flame pattern. Sometimes a blanket of rock-wool material is spread over the sand to create the look of red and orange embers.

The wood has gotten pretty clever, too. Molded from natural wood and available in several species (so you can buy one that might match the wood in the backlot), it even has bark, surface imperfec-tions, and ax marks.

But are all these bells and whistles enough to convince wood-burners to go with gas? Certainly relying on the utility company does not spell self-sufficiency. At the end of the month, there is no such thing as free gas but you can always find free wood. And for those of us who enjoy the physical process of getting wood, building a fire, and yes, even tending it (we're beginning to wonder if we aren't closet pyromaniacs), gas just doesn't cut it. Seeing a gas fireplace out of operation is kind of like going through a Disney World ride with all the machines off and the lights on. Gas is truly the cubic zirconia of woodburning.

There is also a debate on how much "cleaner" gas is than wood. The gas people say that it burns more cleanly than any other source of energy. True, it does not produce smog. What it does produce is carbon dioxide, one of the culprits that causes the greenhouse effect. And increasing your reliance on fossil fuels is never really a good thing—gas, as far as we know, is finite.

But all that said and done, say you go ahead with gas. What now? Let's suppose, like most people, that you want energy efficiency and good looks, too. Here's how to get it.

LOG SETS

The easiest way to go with gas is to add a log set to your masonry fireplace or factory-built metal fireplace. Once a gas line is extended into the firebox, the gas burner system is attached and the logs are placed on a support grate. Then just hit a button, and voilà.

While a lot of these units are still for looks only, there are some that can kick out a respectable amount of heat. Look for ones that feature a fan-driven heat exchanger to circulate and warm the room air. Depending on the design and your fireplace, it can generate up to 30,000 BTUs (British Thermal Units), a number that rivals many freestanding heaters. Expect to pay about $400 for a nice but basic kit.

GAS FIREPLACES

You need more than a new set of perma-logs to add to your fireplace. You need, well, a new fireplace and want to go with gas. Sometimes people arrive at this decision out of necessity—some models can be vented directly through any outside wall, eliminating

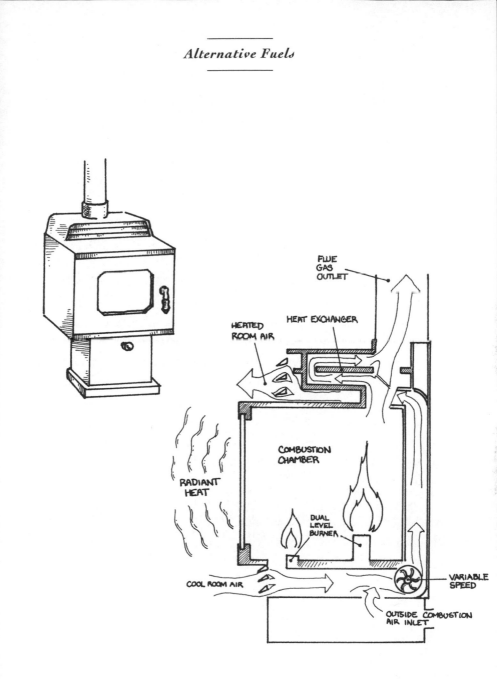

FLUE
GAS
OUTLET

HEAT EXCHANGER

HEATED
ROOM AIR

COMBUSTION
CHAMBER

RADIANT
HEAT

DUAL
LEVEL
BURNER

VARIABLE
SPEED

COOL ROOM AIR

OUTSIDE COMBUSTION
AIR INLET

Typical gas fireplace & parts

the need for a chimney system. Sometimes people see it as a smart way to recoup an investment—you get about a 97% return on what you spend at resale.

The good news is that there are a lot of fireplaces that convert more than 66% of the fuel they consume into heat energy (we found some all the way up to 75%). Granted, you'll never be able to crank up a gas model and get the output you enjoyed from your woodstove, but a little detective work will help you separate the efficiency-winners from the gas-appliance losers.

The tricky part comes when you go to collect information on heat output. When we tried it, we suddenly found ourselves in the land of the nebulous "venting decorative gas appliances." These units are designed to look awfully pretty but perform, well, awfully. Since they are classified as "decorative," they are not required to have performance ratings or to comply with standard tests. (One manufacturer's rep guessed it to be about 25%.) Pass.

Next came the lowest-cost option, the metal box with gas logs and small burner (14,000 to 20,000 BTUs). Taken over the entire heating season, you'll be losing more out the flue opening than you will radiate into the room.

There are things you can do to improve this. The first thing would be to get an automatic flue damper. Usually reserved for larger models (30,000 to 50,000 BTUs), these dampers will cut the opening down to about 15%, providing all the venting you usually need.

Next, look for a heat-exchanging system. Room air will go in at the bottom, circulate in the firebox, then put out at the top. Again, a blower will aid this process and mix the warm air into the cooler room air. A good system should have a thermal sensor to control this process automatically.

Finally, search for a unit that has interior baffling, a feature most of us associate with woodstoves, to force the exhaust air to pass over more surface before it goes up the flue. This will increase the amount of heat you can garner from the exchanger.

Doors are a popular feature but actually work against you if they're left closed while burning, since the radiant heat will be trapped. Doors are only useful when outside air is brought in for combustion (as with a direct-vent gas fireplace). If you do buy a model with doors, look for a single-pane door or two one-piece hinged doors, as opposed to double bi-fold doors.

There are also a few models that resemble thin-profile woodstoves. They project out about a foot and a half from the fireplace surround, and allow greater heat transfer. Such a model will increase your heat efficiency up to the fabled 75% range.

Whatever model unit you get, with whatever kinds of extras, plan on spending about $1,000 (which can climb quickly to $2,000) and another $200 on installation.

DIRECT-VENT GAS FIREPLACES

A number of manufacturers are offering direct-vent fireplaces. They differ from regular gas fireplaces in that they are sealed combustion units. This means that air is piped in from the outside, fed into an airtight combustion chamber, and vented out again. One miracle of combustion is that you don't need a chimney. Most of these units can vent right out the wall behind them but can be run up to the ceiling should you want to install one between two rooms.

This is a good choice for anyone who lives in a too-tight house or is concerned about indoor air pollution. Since all the combustion occurs in a contained unit, there is no danger of by-products being drawn indoors.

Look for units with pilot lights that will shut the unit off or down once things heat up, and a multisetting knob that allows you to control the increments of heat. A well-insulated unit with 75% efficiency will heat about 600 to 1,100 square feet so you'll be able to keep one area toasty while some unused rooms stay cooler.

The one great complaint about these units is the color of the flame. As the efficiency increases, the golden cast will diminish. Some manufacturers have invented clever devices that will colorize the flame. (These devices may need to be replaced after extended use; be sure to check.) The bottom line is: Check the unit out in the store before you get disappointed at home. If the flame color is important, you don't want to end up with a unit that has all the charm of your range.

🔥

Be sure that any gas appliance you buy is certified by the American Gas Association or the Canadian Gas Association.

🔥

Also check that it has a device to prevent gas or LP from entering your home. This can happen when a downdraft extinguishes the pilot light. Most units come equipped with a downdraft diverter or a pilot light shutoff to cut the gas supply once the pilot is out. Be sure you know how yours works.

PELLETS

If you've been investigating alternatives to wood lately, you've probably heard a lot about pellets. What exactly are pellets? Probably, the jewel of the alternative-energy-resources crown. This industry is literally on fire. Pellets, in the generic sense, are cylinders of waste products that have been compressed for reuse as a fuel.

It all started a few years back when entrepreneurs in the Northwest began turning scrap wood from lumber mills into "pelletized firewood." Because these pellets contained only 3% moisture, they were capable of burning very cleanly. (Most burn now with an incredibly low 0.5 grams of particulate an hour, and have over 80% efficiency.) A ton of pellets had about the same heating value as a cord and a half of wood, and cost only about $80.

The problem became, of course, what do you burn this ton of pellets in? A specially designed stove had to be invented. What about two dozen manufacturers have come up with works basically like this: You pour a bag or two of these pellets (about 80 pounds) into a hopper at the top of the stove. The pellets are then fed into an auger system. This auger relies on computers and circuitry to transfer the pellets at a preset rate into the burn pot. Then a combustion fan directs the air to mix with the pellets and a flame to create a clean, hot (about 2,000°) fire. Another fan then carries the heated air out into the room.

The biggest selling point of these units, obviously, is cleanliness. Combustion is so complete that your neighbors won't even know you're burning—there isn't even any visible smoke. And the only flue you need is a small class-L vent (like that used for a natural gas furnace) or a class-B chimney (to vent through the wall like a clothes dryer). You'll also need electricity to run the auger and fans, but that amounts to no more energy than is required to run a 100-watt bulb.

After you've enjoyed your new pellet stove for the season, be sure to empty the hopper and feed system of any leftover pellets. Once summer hits, the high humidity will cause the pellets to absorb moisture, and will sometimes rust expensive metal parts. Call a chimney sweep for a full after-season cleaning and have him bag the extra for summer storage.

Another plus is the relative ease with which pellet stoves operate. All you need to do is turn them on and fill them with pellets. The pellets need to be refilled, of course, but even the hungriest units need to be fed only once every 15 hours. Some need to be fed only twice a week! Most models now come with a thermostat so the heat output is regulated and you don't get the "just-stepped-off-the-plane-in-Florida" feeling you have with most woodstoves. Even without the thermostat, pellet stoves generally provide very even heat, since the flow of fuel is so well-controlled.

Installation is more versatile, too, and less expensive than for cord-wood-burning appliances. Since the sides stay cool (which is good if you have kids running around), the unit can be installed with little clearance. And many do vent through any outside wall, which means you can stick them on any side of the house without worrying about chimney placement. For those set on an insert, some makers have come out with models for both masonry and factory-built fireplaces.

For anyone who enjoys woodburning per se, pellet stoves are going to be a big disappointment. Unlike with gas, you'll never fool anybody at 5 yards that you've got a wood fire burning in there. If you value a cozy, gathering-the-family-around-the-hearth atmosphere, this may not be for you.

Pellet stoves don't exactly spell self-sufficiency, either. Even if you don't count running out for pellets, those (not-so-silent) parts also need electricity, which means no power, no fire.

Another negative factor is the regular maintenance these stoves need. For one, the ashes need to be cleaned out on a very regular basis. And with all those moving parts and snazzy gizmos, regular house calls may be needed. Pellet stoves are not a real do-it-yourself project.

PELLET FUEL

When it comes to the future of pellets, even the cutting-edge technology of "white-wood" (sawdust and shavings from trees that have debarked), pellets may be edged out by regional materials that will cut the cost to consumers.

Today, nearly all pellet stoves burn best using "low-ash" fuel—that is, fuel with 1% ash or less. It burns hot and efficiently, with little ash and invisible emissions, and contains very few impurities.

The Northwest's supply of white-wood pellet material has been cited as a reason why this technology has been so well received. But it's also why most pellet stoves happen to live there. But that will change. Stovemakers, aware of the vast amounts of fuels in other regions, are adapting their stoves to burn materials such as corncobs from Nebraska, walnut shells from Missouri, sunflower hulls from Minnesota, particleboard "nuggets" from Virginia, a cardboard-wood hybrid from Vermont, and even bits of coal from Washington.

But until these fuels and the units that burn them have been perfected, it's best to feed your stove the diet it was designed for. To give the pellet-fuel industry some standards, the Association of Pellet Fuel Industries and the Fiber Fuels Institute got together and set some guidelines. These standards apply to a 40-lb. bag: One, pellets should measure no wider than ¼″ and longer than 1½″. Two, pellets should have "fines" (particles that slough off from the fuel) of 0.5% or less by weight when passed through a 1/8″ screen. And three, pellets should contain no more than 300 parts per million chlorides (which corrode the unit).

The final subject under these national guidelines is the ash content. This is what separates the "premium"-grade fuel from the "standard"-grade fuel (which is similar to how gas for your car works). Premium wood pellets must be less than 1% ash, while standard may be less than 3% ash.

And like variances in gas, most pellet stoves will work fine with the standard fuel. The only tradeoff is that you'll need to empty the ash more and maintain your machine better. Most pellet-fuel makers print an analysis of the fuel right on the bag so you can compare it against these guidelines, but ask your manufacturer what's best for your particular machine.

THE EXTRAS

Despite all the emphasis up to now, fireplaces are as much form as function. Design has long been a focal point and you should take as much care choosing accessories for your fireplace as you do for the rest of the room. With all the designs available, you really have no excuse for just a basic box.

MANTELS AND SURROUNDS

We've always thought a fireplace without a mantel is akin to a sundae with no cherry—certainly fine on its own but all the better and so much more right and pleasing for the addition.

Much more than just a display shelf, mantels add the cozy feeling of home and hearth, which they are literally part of. Mantels got their start in life as paneling. In early days, entire rooms were done

Decorative mantelpieces

> ✺   TO ERASE SMOKE AND SOOT STAINS *from a brick surround, use a kneaded art eraser.*

up in the rich and fine woodworking that most of us associate with mantels. Later, as tastes (and no doubt economics) evolved, the paneling was confined to just one focal point, the fireplace. Eventually, the paneling became what we think of now, one lone shelf above the fireplace.

As the mantel shrank, it created a space now referred to as the surrounds, the area directly next to the firebox that the mantel frames.

Both of these areas now offer endless design possibilities. By tradition, many surrounds are constructed of brick. While this is a good choice for colonial and traditional decors, the choices of materials can accommodate a wide range of styles. Karen did her apartment fireplace in terra cotta to fit with her Santa Fe interior and has Pewabic pottery (supplied by the arts-and-crafts–inspired Detroit studio) surrounding the fireplace in her upstate New York cabin. Sarah has marble to suit the modern, clean lines of her Connecticut home.

Marble has grown in popularity in recent years. The veining and shading available in reasonable Italian marbles offer palates far beyond the simple white. We've seen pink, green, gray, and beige in addition to the usual black. Any of these do wonders when replacing a brick surround. They bring depth and heft to the whole room.

Also popular are surrounds of slate and stone. Each brings a design sensibility that works well with a variety of room schemes. Tile can also adapt to reflect any design (and is really easy to clean).

Mantels have moved far beyond the traditional mahogany (though we still love to see mahogany and lots of leather sofas in a gentleman's study). Most mantels are made of wood—either stained or painted. Stained mantels are made of wood that can take a finish to add depth and luster (walnut, cherry, maple, poplar, pine, and oak) and cost upward of $300. Paint-grade mantels are designed to get a once-over with the brush, as the wood they are made of is imperfect. Buy paint-grade mantels when you just want the mantelwork to blend seamlessly with the rest of your room.

Some other choices are medium-density fiberboard (which is sometimes blended with real wood), plywood with wood veneer, and our favorite, plaster, all of which give you the opportunity to create mantels that can be incredibly ornate and carved into shapes that echo the room.

While prefabricated mantels are most people's usual choice, a hand-carved mantel is something to behold. What's amazing to us is the craftsmanship that goes into these decorations. While they are costly, custom-made mantels are works of art that can be enjoyed daily. And when considering a hand-carved mantel, please think beyond the traditional period styles. Artists can create something that will keep the integrity of your design as well as reflect your passions or location. For a list of some carvers, please see the Resources section.

You have one last option, and that is getting lucky enough to find a (gently) used mantel. In the Detroit suburb where Karen lived when she was younger, a lot of grand old homes were in the process of being torn down. She often went hunting for treasures before these homes were demolished. Many still had the mantels in place.

🕊 TO CLEAN BRICK, *use a mixture of one cup of laundry flakes, four cups of hot water, half a pound of powdered pumice, and half a cup of ammonia. Apply the mixture as sparingly as possible and use gloves.*

If you know of a house that is being destroyed, you may want to see about obtaining the rights to remove the mantel. While this will require careful work, if you are determined, you may just get the mantel of your dreams.

If you don't want to leave so much to chance, check the Resources section for the used-mantel man—Rudy Rzeznikiewicz—or check your city for a shop that specializes in old mantels. Though the structure of what you may find can be lacking, you will find things that go beyond the ordinary. If you like the look of it, it really doesn't matter if it is hand-carved or merely applied jesso—except when you hit the price, since the best mantels can cost $10,000 and even much more.

FIRE TOOLS

Most fire tools come in something called firesets. These sets comprise a shovel, brush, tongs, and a poker (there is also such a thing as a fire suite, which includes a firescreen and andirons).

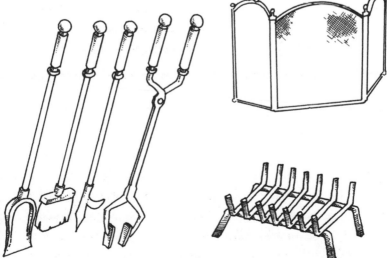

A fireplace suite

Most styles are offered in solid brass (which can cost from $200 to $600), triple-plated brass (which is usually over an iron and zinc base and costs about $150), pewter, or cast iron (up from $100). While effective at prodding your fire and perhaps one day clubbing a nemesis, typical fire-tool designs can be a bit too stuffy for some.

For those who have graduated beyond the brass ball or duck head, the land of fire tools can be a bit challenging. But fear not, many ironworkers and artists have ventured into the design of fire tools (some artists worth a look are listed in the Resources section). We've seen wonderful work in this area as well—everything from tools topped with art glass to carvings of Indian symbols.

If you are on a budget, or a lover of all things old as we are, check antique stores and auction houses. We've been to hundreds of auctions and over half have had fireplace tools up for sale. Most of the older styles are cast iron and go for $50 to $100 unless they have some special significance.

🌿 TO KEEP FIREPLACE TOOLS GLEAMING, *wipe them with a soft cloth that has been dampened with kerosene. Allow the tools to dry before using them.*

ANDIRONS

The objects on which you rest the wood when making a fire, andirons commonly fall into the same category as fire tools. They can be bought in styles that match the design of your tools (most new andirons run about $200 a set for solid brass). Again, it is worth looking into speciality shops and artists' galleries for unique designs. Also remember…check antique stores and auctions for great shapes at good prices.

FIRE SCREENS

Fire screens are another area in which your style can have a big influence. While most of us are happy with the standard mesh you pull across (a draw screen), there are such things out there as a folding screen, a panel screen (which is a single piece you place in front of the fire), a glass-door panel screen, and finally a fan screen (which looks like a large ladies' fan splayed in front of your fireplace). Each of these can run you upward of $200 (with most in the $300 to $400 range), adding a different twist and shape to your fireplace.

> ❦ TO KEEP A SCREEN SLIDING EASILY, *run a candle stub along the track.*

HEARTHS

The area that extends out into the room from the firebox floor, the hearth can be done in much the same way as the surround. Often designers choose to use the same materials for both if the flooring itself is not heat resistant. Most builders choose to have the hearth extend about 24–36" from the edge of the fireplace.

Should you have a wood floor next to the fire, you may want to look into purchasing a fire rug. These rugs, treated to take the punishment of having live sparks land on them without catching fire, can be a little unrefined in their appearance, but they are a lot cheaper than a new floor.

FENDERS

Some people like to finish the area at the edge of the hearth by installing a fender. Metal, shaped around all the sides, fenders are purely decorative and can be great for showing off a beautiful piece of metalwork. Some fenders are made of wood, especially antique American fenders; some even feature seating on the top of them.

Brass fenders can be bought new for about $300 for simple ones to $1,200 for versions with padding on the ends. The best fenders are found through antique dealers and auctions. As fenders are usually pieces crafted for decoration rather than function, don't plan on finding one cheap. If you do, snap it up; it will always be something that will "make" a room. (And then tell us where you found it and if there were any more.)

WOODBOXES

You can use just about anything to hold your wood. There are really two schools of thought on this. Some people like to use a heat-conductive metal so that the wood warms and can be kept close to the fire with no risk of ignition. Some objects we've seen in use are old copper pails, cast-iron coal buckets, and old cooking vessels.

Other people like to keep wood in objects that resemble furniture. The possibilities here are endless. Karen uses a child's toybox near one of her fireplaces. We've seen old blanket boxes, crates from defunct maple syrup suppliers, old tack boxes, even baskets lined with Navaho blankets.

SUMMER USES

Without a fire burning in it, a fireplace becomes a literal black hole in your living room come warm weather. What to do, what to do.

We adore painted fireboards. They can be either very whimsical (a friend has a fireboard with cacti on it, another a rooster) or a trompe l'oeil or something pretty (a depiction of flowers in a basket seems to pop up a lot).

Another option, of course, is actually putting a basket with dried flowers in front of it (dried hydrangeas will last the season and have ample fullness).

But try the unusual. Large porcelain vases look striking when paired with stone or brick. Karen's mother was partial to putting an old parasol in front of hers. We've also seen small screens (carved wooden ones that aren't meant for the sparks, of course) and drying racks with flowers. And we'll never forget the friend of ours who picked up two 3'-high metal hounds that sat staring at each other on either side of the hearth (the mantel set them off perfectly).

Should you be short on fireboards (they are something to look out for on your auction or antique-shopping jaunts), parasols, flowers, large dogs, or a couple of nicely stacked birch logs are also known to do just fine.

9

SOME FINAL THOUGHTS:

Good smells and bad popcorn

Fires have a wonderful woodsy smell when first lit, but for those who like a delicious aroma to fill the house, there are many scenters to toss in once the blaze is roaring and there are even a few that can get your fire stoked. Be sure to be very careful when adding scenters since, as the saying goes, they add fuel to the fire.

Toss these into your fire anytime you want a wonderful smell:

Twigs and branches from cherry, apple, cedar, juniper, pinyon, mesquite, orange, pecan, or hickory trees
Apple or pear cores
Orange or lemon peels
Cinnamon sticks or whole nutmegs
Walnut shells

FIRECONES

Not only do these homemade pinecones scent the room, they also add a pretty touch to the fireplace. Arrange them in a decorative metal bucket—the heat will release a small amount of their smell—but be sure to keep the bundle out of range of sparks! Pinecones also make a wonderful gift at Christmastime.

Start with a dozen clean, dry pinecones free of sap and seeds. In a plastic bag, combine thirty or so drops of your favorite scented oil (the kind used to refresh potpourri or place in lamp rings, available at most bath shops and crafts stores) with a few tablespoons of water used as a dilutant. Shake a few pinecones at a time in the bag and repeat this until all the cones are coated. Allow them to dry and store them in an airtight container, or in a metal bucket near the fire.

WAXED FIRECONES

These cones produce a longer-lasting fragrance as the wax melts onto the wood.

Gather a dozen or so clean, dry pinecones. With a needle and thread, attach a loop you can hold easily to one of the top petals.

Melt three or four small scented wax candles in the top portion of a small double boiler lined with a double thickness of foil. When the candles are totally melted, dunk each cone thoroughly in the wax and allow the excess to drip off. The cones can be placed on waxed paper to dry and then dunked again if you wish the smell and color to be more intense. These pinecones can rest by the fire longer, since the wax seals in their good smell.

PINECONE FIRESTARTERS

Place these firestarters underneath logs that are stacked in the Boy Scout formation, toss a little kindling on top, and light the firestarter for a fragrant blaze.

At the garden or crafts store, purchase some of the Dixie-size paper cups that are used to start seeds. Melt a small scented candle into the top of a small double boiler lined with a double thickness of foil. Once the wax has cooled slightly, using two cups for each candle, pour equal amounts of the wax into each of the cups. Gather several miniature clean, dry pinecones and add about six or seven to each cup, until the wax is almost to the top. Let them cool for several hours until the wax hardens and store them in an airtight container.

SCENTED FIREWOOD AND FATWOOD

Fatwood has become a popular, though somewhat costly, choice of kindling. But if you think regular fatwood can get expensive, check the price of scented fatwood in gift stores! While we aren't sure why some folks pay the extra money for something that only lasts about eight minutes, it's so easy to make your own that doing so might be worth your while. For good smells that last longer, this do-it-yourself method can be used on seasoned firewood as well.

Take some of your scented oil, mix it with eight times as much water, and pour the mixture into an old plant mister. Lay out the fatwood on newspaper and lightly spray it. Don't soak the stuff; just give it a light coat and allow it to dry. You can then add scented fatwood to your fire for next to nothing.

SIMMERING WOODSTOVE POTPOURRI

We're sure many woodstove owners love this easy and decorative trick. For those new to the game, simply place a lovely old kettle on top of your lit stove and fill it with water and one of the "simmering potpourri" products on the market (or make your own potpourri from dried orange and lemon peels, cinnamon sticks, and cloves). Just be extra careful not to let all the water evaporate; but we're sure you knew that, too.

POPPING CORN

Most of us remember those long-handled, lidded black saucers from our childhood. An old-fashioned popcorn popper sat in Karen's childhood cottage for as long as she could remember. So when we started writing this book, we decided to find out exactly how you make perfect fireplace popcorn.

We tried it ourselves with not-too-great results. Sometimes it burned, sometimes nothing really happened. We tried to preheat our oil in the fireplace, and then add the corn (even though the pros say you can dump it in all at once). We then tried to preheat the popper in the fireplace and then the oil (that worked better), but the corn would burn because the oil was really hot (though some came out). Desperate, we tried to heat the oil in a pan and heat the popper separately and then dump it all together (this worked sometimes, too).

The times that we did manage to get something, it tasted a bit weird. Maybe we've been spoiled by the microwave—we don't know.

Then we figured maybe our popper was too new and not seasoned enough. So we thought we'd better consult the pros (there are just a few manufacturers that still offer poppers in their product line) and hoped for guidance. They told us just to use a small amount of oil and pop away. That didn't work too well, we told them. So how *do* they do it, precisely?

Well, they told us, they don't. They use the microwave.

Better luck to you.

RESOURCES

ANDIRONS

Elephant Hill Ironworks
RR 1, Box 168
Tunbridge, VT 05077
(802) 889-9444
send $3 for an illustrated brochure

Offers strict reproduction work of 17th- and 18th-century irons.

Jim DeWoody
(516) 324-7980

Irons resemble modern towers, very clean lines, everything is hand-made by a blacksmith at La Forge Francais. About $2,500.

Ian Eddy
RFD 1, Box 975
Putney, VT 05346
(802) 387-5991
send $3 for an illustrated brochure

Custom contemporary work.

Jim MaGee
Sointu, New York

Irons resemble "stacked I beams", very modern. About $225.

FIREPLACE TOOLS

The Antler People
P.O. Box 255
Pinckney, MI 48169
(313) 878-6083

Offers tools with shed antler tops. From $115 for black to $260 for solid brass.

Michele Oka Doner
available at Ted Muehling, New York and the Whitney Museum's The Store Next Door

Tools are branch shapes cast in bronze. About $1,000.

Ann Maes
available at Sointu, New York, and Chiasso, Chicago

Tools are bent steel rods. About $325.

Stone County Ironworks
Mountain View, Arkansas
(800) 223-4722

Tools have a lot of shape and unusual heads. About $350.

MANTELS

John Bryan
39 Milliken Road
North Yarmouth, ME 04097
(207) 829-6447

Bryan does custom-made, handcarved mantels that reflect the taste and interests of its future owner. Gorgeous work by an excellent craftsman. Call or write for more information.

Malcolm MacGregor
Piscataqua Architectural Woodwork Co.
53 Bagdad Rd. RFD 2
Durham, NH 03824
(603) 868-2663

MacGregor does work mostly from the Georgian era utilizing his collection of over 500 antique planes. Can do work that reflects styles popular up until the 1800s when machine tools took over. Works mostly in pine, the wood of choice for that time. Great prices for such wonderful work.

Rudolph Rzeznikiwicz
12 Gorman Rd.
Brooklyn, CT 06234
(203) 774-6759

The used mantel man, Rudy usually has about fifty to one hundred used mantels that he has salvaged from houses due to be destroyed. He also has antique doors and tons of matched and unmatched hinges. Great prices.

REFURBISHING OLD STOVES

"New Life for Old Stoves," by John Vivian. *Mother Earth News*, December/January 1994, Issue #141. To order a back issue, send $5.00 per copy to MEN Back issues, P.O. Box 10941, Des Moines, Iowa 50340-0941.

An excellent step-by-step guide to redoing old stoves for use.

GLOSSARY

baffles
: Metal plates in the body of a wood stove which control the flow of combustible gases (volatiles) that burn and provide additional heat. Baffles also enable more heat to radiate from the stove by forcing the heated air to travel a longer path to the flue outlet. Also called baffle plates.

bucking
: Cutting and splitting wood the correct length and thickness for burning.

BTU.
: (British Thermal Unit). A unit for measuring energy; the amount of energy required to increase the temperature of 1 pound of water by 1 degree Fahrenheit.

chimney capacity
: The maximum safe venting capability of a chimney, expressed in BTU. per hour, and related to the flow of flue gas up a chimney under given conditions of temperature and barometric pressure.

cord
: A standard cord is a pile of wood stacked 4 feet high, 8 feet wide, with logs that are 4 feet long— totaling 128 cubic feet. A face cord is a pile of wood stacked 4 feet high, 8 feet wide, with logs

that are 1–2 feet long. Also called a short cord.

creosote	A sticky liquid which forms when hot smoke vapors come in contact with a cold chimney flue; the substance deposits in the flue and hardens to a tar-like consistency. Burning unseasoned wood causes greater creosote build-up.
damper	An adjustable plate in the flue of a stove or fireplace for controlling the flow of air or draft.
draft	The flow of air into a stove or fireplace and up the chimney.
firebox	The body of a wood stove or fireplace—where the fuel is burned.
firebrick	Brick that can withstand high temperatures and is used to line wood stoves, fireplaces, and chimneys.
fireclay	A heat-resistant clay used in the making of firebrick, it can withstand high temperatures without cracking or deforming.
fireplace insert	A device installed inside a fireplace that covers the fireplace opening, and is meant to extract additional heat from the fire.
flue	The inner lining of a chimney which protects the chimney structure from heat, creosote, carbon deposits, etc. Usually made of a ceramic material.
flue gases	The gases in an operating venting system, consisting of air and combustion products.

fly ash   Ash that goes up the chimney, rather than remaining in the firebox of a fireplace or stove.

green wood   Wood not yet ready for efficient burning because it is unseasoned or damp.

hardwood   Dense, heavy wood that is the most suitable type for fuel because it burns longer, steadier, and with little or no sparking. Ash, maple, birch, etc.

heat exchanger   A chamber on the top of a stove's firebox or installed inside a fireplace which acts as a secondary heat radiator.

kindling   Dry, thin pieces of wood used to start a fire.

maul   A metal wedge used to split large logs.

seasoning   The drying of wood intended for use as fuel.

softwood   Lightweight wood which burns quickly and emits sparks. Generally not suitable for fuel except as kindling. Pine, fir, spruce, etc.

soot   Black, velvety carbon particles which deposit inside chimneys, appliances, and stovepipes, originating from oxygen-poor flames.

stacking   The tendency for air to flow into a house on the lower floors, and out of a house on the upper floors. Caused by the natural buoyancy of warm air and differences in air pressure between the inside of a house and the outside.

stove mat   A prefabricated panel used to protect a floor or wall from excessive heat and sparks.

thimble

A protective metal or fireclay sleeve or cylinder installed in a wall, through which stovepipe passes.

unit

A stack of wood measuring 2 feet by 2 feet, with logs that are 16 inches long.

INDEX